GENESIS

At last, here is a complete and faithful translation of the Genesis Epic. Genealogies have been removed to an appendix, available to the scholar but no longer intruding on the reader's concentration. Words and sentences have been added (easily identified as they appear in a different type font), to explain and clarify, to remove contradictions and maintain the continuity of a simple but exciting story line. This edition of *Genesis* invites all readers, from the religious believer to the neutrally secular, to appreciate why *Genesis* enthralled ancient audiences even before it entered the Holy Canon and was considered to be the word of God.

The explanation of the origins of the universe, the creation of man and woman, the beginning of evil, God's withdrawal from the world and his re-entry into human history to achieve his purposes, all these will stimulate the minds of modern readers who are fascinated by how our ancestors understood the power that created the world and the beginning of human life on this planet.

SIDNEY BRICHTO *is a leading Liberal Jewish Rabbi and theologian who writes and lectures on Jewish, religious and moral issues .*

The People's Bible

Genesis

newly translated by Sidney Brichto

Sinclair-Stevenson

First published in Great Britain by
Sinclair-Stevenson
3 South Terrace, London SW7 2TB

British Library Cataloguing in Publication Data.
A CIP catalogue record for this book is available from
The British Library.

ISBN 0 953 73980 5

Typeset by Rowland Phototypesetting Ltd, Bury St Edmunds, Suffolk.
Printed and bound by Mackays of Chatham plc. Kent.

This new interpretative translation is dedicated to the memory of my brother, Chanan Herbert Brichto. He loved the Bible with enormous passion not for its historical veracity but for its moral and literary genius. His seminal books Towards a Grammar of Political Poetics *and* The Names of God *will, I am convinced, in time revolutionize biblical scholarship. Many of the new insights in the translation of Genesis are based on his scholarship and fertile imagination. His respect, bordering on worship, of those geniuses who were the vehicles of the 'Still Small Voice' of God, is what inspired me to make this attempt to give the Bible back to people of great, little, or no faith.*

I want to thank Christopher Sinclair-Stevenson whose faith in the project never wavered when my own began to ebb. This attempt is as much his creation as mine. I thank Beverley Taylor, my personal assistant for so many years, for her dedication and help in enabling me to fulfil my creative interests; and to my wife and children for their advice and patience in my pursuit of this ambitious project. Finally, to John Porter my own and Christopher's gratitude, for without his vision this Genesis and the accompanying volumes might never have seen the light of day.

SIDNEY BRICHTO

Preface

The simple purpose of this new Bible is to give it back to people who welcome a good story, fine poetry, and inspiration. For too long now, the Bible has become the best-seller least read. There are several reasons for this, foremost among them the claim of believers that the Bible was written or inspired by God. As our age has become increasingly secular such a claim has turned people away. Also, atheists and humanists maintain that the Bible is a pack of distortions and false phophecies which prevent men and women from accepting their full responsibility for human destiny.

Literate people, however, aware of the Bible as a great classic, feel obligated to read it. Most do not get very far. Repetitions, lack of chronological order, tedious genealogical inserts, stories which cry out for explanations which are not given, incomprehensible thoughts – all these elements, as well as the formal divisions into chapters and verses, have forced most readers to give up even before they have reached the middle of the first book of Genesis.

The purpose of this edition of the Bible is to recast it in such a manner as to make it readable. It will be the complete biblical text faithfully translated after reference to other translations. The biblical narrative style is so sparse that it leaves much to the imagination. This provides a challenge to consider what the author has left out. On occasion, the translator will respond by interacting with the text to fill out the story. To avoid confusion, such elaborations will be indicated by a different print font. This is done with the expectation that some readers will feel that they (and indeed they may be right) could have done better. Such reactions are welcome and proof that the editor's objective of making the Bible come alive has been achieved. Material which appears irrelevant and interrupts the flow is moved into an appendix. Words and sentences will be added, also in a different print font, when necessary to provide continuity and to remove seeming contradictions. References will abound, to enable the reader to find the place in a traditional Bible should he or she wish to make comparisons.

Since the Bible is a library of books, each book or group of books will therefore require special treatment, with a specific introduction to explain how the editor has dealt with the material in his attempt to enable you not only to possess a Bible but to read it with comprehension and even with pleasure.

Introduction

Many people have tried to read the entire book of Genesis, but with mixed success. Usually they stop when they can no longer cope with the large chunks of 'begets' which interrupt what has already becoming confusing and difficult.

Before they close the book, they have been captivated by the sudden appearance of God, his creation of the heavens and earth, their creatures and humanity. They have also been excited by Eve's choice of the forbidden fruit by which she stole knowledge from God for her man and her progeny. They carry on to Noah and the flood but begin to find the repetition and even contradictions wearisome. But is is when they encounter all the 'begets' that they lose heart. This, coupled with a lack of comprehension of the lives of the Patriarchs, leads them to give up, with sadness and sometimes guilt at their failure to persevere in completing the book which is recognized to be one of the pillars on which Western civilization rests.

I would ask readers to try again with this edition. As I have said in the Preface, all but a few of the genealogical tables have been put in an appendix for reference, if needed. Words, sentences and even paragraphs have been added in a different print font – to distinguish it from the original – to smooth out contradictions and to make it all comprehensible. Notes are at the foot of the page when the Editor feels that you would require some help in understanding the motives of the author or the skills he employed to make this narrative so popular with his contemporaries and their successors.

Genesis is an epic of grand proportions and is presented in an appropriate format which can be read in a few hours. It is hoped that the easy flow will encourage you not to seek a quick read but to reflect on its subtleties and imagery. The unfolding of a tale which begins with creation and ends with the sons of Jacob settled in Egypt ready to burst out as a nation into history can be read on many levels.

Reading Genesis as literature, one should note the changes in style. There is a greater majesty of prose when God is the hero creating the heavens and earth and fashioning Adam from the dust of the earth in his image. As God moves off centre stage and casts Abraham and his descendants in leadership roles, the prose becomes more human though equally poetic, except at those moments when God intervenes to reveal his awesome power – as when he commands Abraham to sacrifice the son he promised to him and for whom he had waited almost a lifetime. Few classics or modern stories can equal the pathos of Joseph revealing himself to his brothers after their expression of remorse and repentance for what they had done to him.

On a political level, the author sought to create for the Israelites a glorious history which made them believe in their rights to the Promised Land and gave them a pride in their national identity as a people chosen by God. In this he was responding to the needs of his audience in the manner of Shakespeare when the latter enhanced the history of the reigning dynasty.

On a scientific and theological level – and up to Copernicus and Galileo these areas of study were considered to be the same – the author explains the origins of the universe; why humanity is gifted with intelligence but cursed with death and the need to eke out a living from the recalcitrant soil. God needs Adam to share in the enjoyment of his beautiful creation; but, like a robot who learns how to achieve independence from his programmer, Man becomes a challenge to God. Frustrated by human perversity from the time that Cain kills his brother Abel, God finally destroys the earth, sparing only Noah and his family and pairs of animals to keep the world going.

But God realizes that 'Man is evil from his youth' and that he can no longer continue to play roulette with the world because of human wickedness. He withdraws from the role of leading actor to become the Director of human history when he chooses one man, Abraham, to become his representative on earth in his attempt to improve human society through obedience to his moral laws.

All these layers intertwine to make a complex story in which evey human emotion – love, hate and jealousy – is revealed on the most elemental and profound levels. If William Shakespeare at the height of his genius can make us believe that he was the mind of God, the author of Genesis at the height of his power reveals the heart and soul of God.

When the reader comes across immoral behaviour on the part of the heroes of Genesis – sometimes condoned by God – let him be wary of feeling disgust because it is a holy book. When Genesis was written, when the author tapped the mythological sources of the ancient world and drew upon certain national memories to write his work of genius, he was not writing a holy book, he was writing an epic which he hoped would mesmerise his audience and win him their approval. To achieve this, his characters had to be imbued with a human mixture of good and evil, cowardice and courage, and all those other emotional polarities which rule the human heart and mind.

His success is proved by the fact that, thousands of years later, his work is in every home. The objective behind this edition of Genesis is that it will not only be owned but also read.

The Name of God

The name of God as it appears in the Bible is YHVH (Hebrew script has no vowels). This is the ineffable name which was always read as Adonai, meaning 'my Lord'. The traditional translation of YHVH is therefore Lord. The Jerusalem Bible translation refers to God as Yahweh which most scholars believe was the pronunciation of the four consonants. I was tempted to follow this example, because the name makes God into a vital personality – the real hero of *Genesis*: creator, monitor and judge of humanity – rather than an abstract force. Cautious respect for tradition made me hold to 'the Lord', but I hope that the reader will remember that the Lord, the God of Israel, is portrayed as a personality revealing the full range of emotions; paternal justice, maternal compassion, love and reason, regret and anger, punishing and forgiving.

Index of major episodes

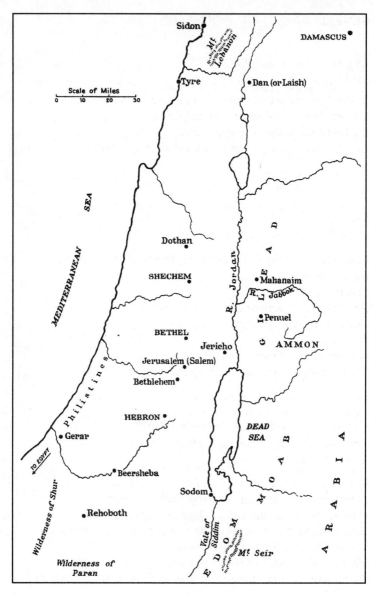

W<small>HEN,</small>
In the beginning God created the heavens and the earth,
The world was turbulent without form,
Darkness permeated the deep abyss,
And the breath of God was blowing over the water face,

God said, "Let there be light" and it was light.
God saw the light. It was good.
God made a division between light and darkness.
God called the light – day and the darkness he called night.
Thus passed the evening and morning of the first day.

God said, "Let there be a dome in the midst of the waters to
Divide the layers of water."
God made the dome, thus
Dividing the waters under the dome from
The waters over the dome.
So it was.
God called the dome – The Heavens
Thus passed the evening and morning of the second day.

God said, "Let the waters under the heavens join together
In one place so that dry land can be seen."
So it was. God called the dry land – earth.
The joining of the waters he called – the seas.
God saw that it was good.

God said, "Let the earth bring forth vegetation,
Plants which bear their own reproductive seed;
Fruit trees producing fruit of their own species
Replenishing the earth with their own seed." It was so:
The earth sprouted forth vegetation,
Plants making seed of their own kind;
All varieties of trees producing fruit with their seeds in them.

God saw: It was good.
Thus passed the evening and the morning of the third day.

God said: "Let there be balls of fire in the heavenly dome.
To distinguish between day and night,
To be used as signs, to tell the seasons, days and years;
Let the lights in the heavenly dome give light to the earth!"
So it was, when God forged the two great lights,
The greater light to hold sway over the day,
The lesser light to hold sway over the night,
Together with the stars.
Thus God placed them in the dome of heaven,
To give light to the earth,
To hold sway over day and night and
To distinguish between light and darkness.
God saw: it was good.
Thus passed the evening and the morning of the fourth day.

God said, "Let the waters teem with swarms of living creatures,
Let birds fly on earth and on the face of the dome of heaven."
So God created great sea monsters and all crawling
Living creatures with which the waters swarm,
In their various shapes; and all kinds of winged creatures.
God saw it was good.
God blessed them with these words,
"Be fruitful, increase in numbers, fill the waters of the seas
And let the birds increase upon the earth."
Thus passed the evening and the morning of the fifth day.
God said, "Let the earth bring forth every type of creature,
Cattle, creeping things, all kinds of wild animals."
So it was.
God made all types of wild beasts and cattle –
All the varieties of animals that crawl on earth.
God saw: it was good.
God said: "Let us make man in our image to look like us
Let him rule over the fish of the sea,
The birds of the heavens, the cattle,

The whole earth, all the creatures who creep upon the land."
So God created man in his image.
In the shape of God, he created him.
Male and female, he created them.
God blessed them; he said to them:
"Be fruitful, increase and fill the earth,
Conquer her and rule over the fish of the sea,
The birds of the heavens
Every creature that crawls on the earth."
God said: "I have given you every seed-bearing plant
On the face of the earth and
Every tree with seed-bearing fruit.
This shall be your food.
To all the animals of the earth; to all the birds of heaven,
To all who creep upon the earth, which have life in them,
I give the foliage of plants for food."
So it was. God saw all that he had done,
It was very good!
Thus passed the evening and the morning of the sixth day.

The heavens, the earth – all creation was completed.
On the seventh day God completed the work he was doing.
He rested on the seventh day from all the work he had done.
God blessed the seventh day and made it holy
Because on that day, he rested from all his labour which
God in his creativity had fulfilled.
This is the story of the heavens and the earth –
How they were created.

He blew into his nostrils the breath of life

On the day when the LORD God made heaven and earth,[1]
Before there were plants of the field on earth and
Before there was any foliage growing in the fields,

[1] This is either an elaboration of the creation of Adam and the animal world or an alternative version.

For the Lord God had not yet given rain to the earth,
There was no one to work the land,
A mist came forth from the earth
To water the entire land surface.
The LORD God formed Man[1]
From the dust of the ground.
He blew into his nostrils
The breath of life
Thus Man became a living creature.
The LORD God planted a garden in Eden which is in the east.
There he placed Man whom he had formed.
The LORD God made to shoot up from the ground
All kinds of trees to delight the eyes and good for fruit.
The tree of life was in the midst of the garden,
Also the tree that yields knowledge of good and evil.
A river flowed from the east to water the garden;
From there it divided itself into four streams.
The name of the first is Pishon.
It encircles the whole land of the Havilah,
Where there is much gold.
The gold of that land is good.
There, you will also find bdellium and onyx stone.
The name of the second river is Gihon.
It encircles the entire land of Cush.
The name of the Third river is Hidekel [Tigris].
It flows east of Assyria.
The fourth river is the Euphrates.
God took Man and rested him in the garden of Eden
To work it and to keep it.

The LORD God commanded Man, saying,
"You may eat from all the trees of the garden,
But from the tree yielding knowledge of good and evil
Do not eat from it.

---

[1] When *adam* is preceded by the definite article *ha*, I translate it as Man because *ha-adam* is a variant of *ha-ish* [man].

"Because when you eat of it, you will surely die."
The LORD God said: "It is not good for Man to be alone!
Let me make him a helpmate."
So the LORD God formed out of the ground
All the animals of the field and all the birds of heaven.
He brought them to Man to see what he would name them.
Whatever names Man gave to the living creatures,
Those are their names to this very day.
Man gave names to all the cattle, the birds of the heavens,
The animals of the wild,
But Adam, himself, did not find a suitable helpmate.

The LORD God caused a deep sleep to come over Man.
As he slept, he took one of his ribs, but closed up the
Flesh in its place.
The LORD built out of the rib which he had taken from Man
A woman, and he brought her to Man.
Man said: "This is good.
Bone of my bones
Flesh of my flesh
Let this one be called woman [ishah]
Because this has come out of man [ish]."
Thus, a man will leave his father and mother,
Clings unto his wife, and they
Become one flesh.
Both of them were naked,
Man and his wife.
They felt no shame.

The serpent was the slyest of all the animals of the wild
Which the LORD God had made.
Taking advantage of her innocence, he said to the woman,
"Is it not that God has said,
'Do not eat from all the trees of the garden?'"
The woman replied to the serpent:
"No, we may eat from the fruit of the trees of the garden, but
From the fruit of the tree which is in the centre of the garden

God said, 'Do not eat from it, nor touch it, lest you die.'"
The serpent said to the woman, "Nonsense, you will not die!
He has told you this because he knows that when you eat of it,
Your eyes will be opened.
You will be like God
Experiencing good and evil."
The woman saw that the fruit of the tree was ready to eat.
It cried out to be eaten.
Not only that but the tree had the power to make one wise;
She took one of its fruit and she ate. **She did not die**.

So she gave it to her man who now was with her and he ate.
Instantly, the eyes of both of them were opened.
They realised that they were naked.
They sewed fig leaves together and made themselves loincloths.
They heard the sound of the LORD God strolling in the garden
In the cool of the day.
The man and woman hid from the face of the LORD God
Behind the trees of the garden.
But the LORD God called Man and asked him:
"Where are you?"
He replied: "I heard the sound of you in the garden
And I was frightened because I was naked and I hid."
God said, "Ah, who told you that you were naked?
It can only be that from the one tree I commanded
You not to eat, you have eaten!"
Man **to justify himself** said,
"It is the woman whom you gave to be with me –
It is she who gave me from the tree, so I ate."

The LORD God reprimanded the woman,
"What is this that you have done?"
The woman answered,
"The serpent seduced me and I ate."
The LORD God said to the serpent,
"Because you did this,
You are cursed more than any beast or

The animals of the wild.
On your belly you will crawl and
Dust will you eat all the days of your life.
A fearsome hatred will I put between you and the woman,
Between your descendants and hers.
He will crush your head,
You will strike his heel."
To the woman, he said,
"I will greatly increase the labour of your childbearing,
In pain you will bear children,
But nonetheless you will sexually desire your husband,
And he will be your master." To Man, he said,
"Because you listened to your woman's voice and
You ate from the tree of which I commanded you not to eat,
Because of you, the ground will be cursed.
With painful labour will you eat of its produce
All the days of your life.
Thorns and thistles will she bring forth for you,
You shall eat of the shrubs of the field.
By the sweat of your brow you will eat bread
Until you return to the ground
Because from it you were taken,
Because dust you are,
To dust will you return."
Now that the man had eaten of the tree of knowledge,
He desired her and knew that she would bear him
children.
Man named his wife Eve [Havah] because
She would be the mother of all human life.
God made for Man and wife clothing of skin,
And he dressed them.

The LORD God said, "See Man has become like one of us
Knowing good and evil.
Now, **though I have deprived him of immortality,**
What if he were to thrust out his hand and

Take also of the tree of life and eat of it and live forever.
There would be no difference between him and us.
He would have knowledge and be immortal,
Whereas before he ate of the tree of knowledge
He was immortal but without knowledge."
So the LORD God thrust him out of the Garden of Eden
To work the ground from which he was taken.
He chased Man out and caused him to dwell east of Eden –
Cherubim and a revolving flaming sword guarded
The path to the tree of life.

Am I my brother's keeper?

Man lay with Havah, his wife,
She conceived and bore him Cain [Acquired].
She named him thus because she said,
"I have acquired a man child from the Lord."
She said, "God has cursed me with mortality
But has given me issue,
Through my children I will be immortal."
She bore again his brother, Abel[1]
Abel was a shepherd, and Cain was a tiller of the soil.
After some time, Cain brought an offering to the LORD
From the fruits of the ground.
Also, Abel brought from the first born of his flocks,
And their fattest parts.
The Lord preferred Abel and his offering.
Cain and his offering he did not favour.
Cain was very angry and his face fell in deep sadness.
The LORD said to Cain, "Why are you so sad?
Why is your face downcast?

---

[1] The author does not tell us who named Cain's brother Abel. The Hebrew name *Hevel* means "vanity" or "futility". No mother would give her child such a name. This is a sure indication that the tale of Cain's murder of Abel – the man who was not to have a destiny – is a metaphor to give a moral lesson: whenever one kills a fellow man, he is killing his brother.

Consider, if you improve, you will be favoured.
If you do not improve, sin is like a snake at the door.
Its desire is for you, but you must master it!"
Cain was thinking about Abel his brother.
When they were in the field together
Cain turned on Abel his brother and killed him.
The LORD said to Cain,
"Where is Abel, your brother?"
He replied, "I do not know.
Am I my brother's keeper?"
He demanded, "What have you done?
The sound of your brother's blood
Cries out to me from the ground!"
Now, cursed are you by the ground
Which opened its mouth to swallow
The blood of your brother, dripping from your hands.
When you till the soil, it will no longer
Yield to you its riches.
You will be a wanderer and a fugitive on the earth
Looking for sustenance.
Cain cried out to the LORD,
"The punishment for my sin is beyond bearing,
Look, today, you have chased me out from the face of the
    earth,
And from your presence am I hidden.
I will become a wanderer and a fugitive on the earth,
So it will be that anyone who finds me will kill me."
The LORD said to him, "Therefore, I say anyone who kills Cain
Will be avenged sevenfold."
The LORD put a mark on Cain
To prevent him being smitten by anyone finding him.
So Cain left the presence of the LORD
And dwelt in the Land of Nod, east of Eden.
Cain lay with his wife; she conceived and bore him Enoch.
He built a city and he called the city Enoch, after his son.
Enoch had a son Irad.

Irad had a son Mehujael.
Mehujael had a son Metushael.
Metushael had a son Lamech.
Lamech took two women,
The name of the first was Adah,
The name of the second Zillah.
Adah gave birth to Jabal.
He was the first to dwell in tents looking after livestock.
The name of his brother was Jubal.
He was the first to play the lyre and the flute.
Zillah bore Tubal Cain,
The first to hammer bronze and iron.
Tubal Cain's sister was Naamah.
Lamech boasted to his women, Adah and Zillah,
"Hear my voice, O women of Lamech,
Give heed to my speech.
I killed a man for wounding me,
A youth for bruising me.
If Cain is avenged sevenfold
Then Lamech is avenged seventy and sevenfold."

Adam lay with his wife again and she bore a son
She called his name Seth because she said:
"God has given me another child in place of Abel
Because Cain killed him."
Seth also fathered a son whom he named Enosh.
Then mankind began to invoke God by the name of Yahweh.[1]

The ten generations from Adam to Noah

This is Adam's genealogical table
From the time God created Adam
In God's likeness, he created him.
Male and female he created them.

---

[1] Yahweh, inaccurately transliterated as 'Jehovah', is normally translated as the Lord. See introductory note on the name of God.

He blessed them and called them Adam [man]
When he created them from the ground [adamah]

1. Adam was 130 years when he sired a son
   In his own likeness and form; he named him Seth.
   He sired other sons and daughters and lived for 930 years.
2. Seth sired Enosh when he was 105.
   He sired sons and daughters and lived for 912 years.
3. Enosh sired Kenan when he was 90.
   He sired other sons and daughters. He lived for 905 years.
4. Kenan sired Mehalalel when he was 70.
   He sired sons and daughters and lived for 910 years.
5. Mehalalel was 65 when he sired Jared.
   He sired sons and daughters and lived for 895 years.
6. Jared was 162 when he sired Enoch.
   He sired sons and daughters and lived for 962 years.
7. Enoch was 65 when he sired Methuselah.
   He walked with God and sired sons and daughters.   He
   lived 365 years.
   Enoch walked with God.
   Suddenly he vanished because God had taken him.
8. Methuselah was 187 when he sired Lamech.
   He sired sons and daughters and lived for 969 years.
9. Lamech was 182 when he sired a son.
   He named him Noah, prophesying:
   "He will comfort us for our labours
   And the painful toil of our hands
   On the earth which the Lord has cursed."
   He sired sons and daughters and lived for 777 years.
10. Noah was 500 years old when he sired
    Shem, Ham and Japheth.

And it came to pass,
As human creatures filled the earth and
Daughters were born to them,
The sons of God saw that they were lovely to look at.
They seized whatever women they liked.

The LORD, **fearful that their offspring would share
In the immortality of the gods**, said:
"My eternal breath will not endure in Man forever
In that he is but mortal flesh, let his years be 120."
Demigods dwelt on earth in those days.
Especially afterwards when the sons of God
Cohabited with the daughters of men and gave them children.
These were the giants who were recorded in history
As the heroes of old.

The Lord regretted that he had created Man on earth

The LORD saw how exceedingly evil was Man on the earth.
The inclinations of his heart
Were nothing but wicked
All the day long.
The LORD regretted that he had created Man on earth,
And his heart broke with grief.
The LORD decided, "I will wipe out Man
Whom I have created from the face of earth.
Everything – Man and beast,
The reptiles and the birds of the sky –
Because I regret that I made them **for men to rule**."
Noah alone found grace in the LORD's sight.

This is the story of Noah:
Noah was a straight-forward man,
An honest man among his contemporaries.
Noah walked humbly with God.
Noah sired three sons; Shem, Ham and Japheth.
The Earth was destroying itself before God.
The Earth was bursting with lawlessness.
God again looked upon the earth.
It was self-destructive for every species of flesh
Had perverted its way on the earth.

God informed Noah: "I see before me the end of all flesh
Because the land is overwhelmed with their lawlessness.
So, I will now destroy them together with the land.
But you and your sons I will spare,
This is what you must do.
Make yourself an ark of gopher-wood; make rooms in the ark.
To prevent leakage – caulk it inside and out with pitch.
This is how to construct it:
300 cubits the ark's length,
50 cubits its width and
30 cubits its height.
You should provide window light in the ark,
A cubit between it and the ceiling.
The door of the ark should be on its side.
In this manner, you shall build a lower, second and third floor.
As for myself, I am preparing a flood of water for the earth
To destroy all flesh from under the heavens,
In which is the breath of life.
Everything on earth will die.
But I will make my covenant with you.
You will enter the ark,
You, your sons, your wife and your daughters-in-law with you.
From all that lives and from all flesh,
Two of each you will bring into the ark
To keep alive with you, one male and one female.
All the varieties of birds and beasts,
Of all the species that creep on land
Two of each will at my command come to you to be kept alive.
As for you, take all kinds of food which you require.
Make enough stores, so that you and they will have food.
Noah did exactly as God commanded him. So he did.

When the ark was completed, the LORD instructed Noah,
"Now board the ark, you and all your family; yes, you alone of
This generation have I in my judgement found righteous.
In addition to what I have already told you,

Of every clean animal, **which is permitted for food**
And for offerings to me, admit seven pairs, male and female.
But, as I commanded earlier,
Of unclean animals, only two –
Male and female; also of the birds of heaven, seven pairs
Male and female, to preserve life on the face of the earth.
As for me, in seven days' time,
I will rain down upon the earth for forty days and forty nights.
I will blot out every creature which I have made
From off the face of the earth."
And Noah obeyed the LORD in every matter.

Noah was six hundred years old when the flood began and the
Waters covered the earth. Noah, his sons,
His wife and his sons' wives began to board the ark
Before the onslaught of the waters of the flood.
From the clean and the unclean animals; from the fowl,
From everything that trod and crept upon the earth.
Two by two **by divine order** they came to Noah, to the ark,
Male and female just as God had commanded Noah.
So it was that, at the end of seven days,
The waters of the deluge covered the earth.
In the six hundredth year of Noah's life,
On the seventeenth day of the second month,
On that very day, all the fountains of the great deep burst.
The windows of heaven were opened.
Rain poured down for forty days and forty nights.
On that very day Noah, Shem, Ham and Japheth,Noah's sons,
The wife of Noah and the three wives of his sons with him,
Entered the ark, **never again to return to their homes:**
They and all wild beasts of every kind,
Domestic cattle of every sort,
Every type of creature which creeps on the ground,
Flying birds of all kinds, every bird, anything with wings.
They came to Noah's ark, two by two from all flesh
In which resided the breath of life.

Those who came were male and female; of all flesh they came.
Just as God commanded him.
Then the LORD closed him in.

When the flood had been on the earth for forty days,
The water increased and lifted up the ark
So it rose high above the ground.
The waters swelled mightily, so much on the earth that
The ark bobbed up and down on the waters.
The waters were so great on the earth that they
Covered the highest mountains everywhere under the skies.
Fifteen cubits higher did the water surge.
The mountains were overwhelmed.
All flesh that crept on earth died –
Fowl, cattle, wild beasts and everything which
Swarmed upon the earth, and every human being.
Everything which had the breath of life in its nostrils,
All that was on dry land died.
So did he blot out all existence
On the earth's surface, from mankind to cattle,
From reptiles to the fowl of the heaven,
They were wiped off the earth.
Only Noah and those with him in the ark were left alive.

After the flood had overwhelmed the earth for
One hundred and fifty days God remembered Noah and
All the beasts and cattle with him in the ark.
God caused a wind to blow over the earth,
The waters began to subside.
He closed up the fountains of the deep
And the windows of heaven.
The rain from heaven was contained.
The waters slowly subsided on the land.
Thus, at the end of one hundred and fifty days,
The waters diminished.
On the seventeenth day of the seventh month
The ark anchored itself among the hills of Ararat.

The waters continued to lessen until the tenth month.
On the tenth day of the month, the hill tops could be seen.
At the end of forty days, Noah opened the window of the ark.
He sent forth a raven who flew back and forth from the ark
Until the water dried up on the land.
Then he sent out a dove to see whether the
Water had eased up from covering the ground's surface.

The dove could not find a place to perch
So she returned to him into the ark
Because waters were still covering the whole earth.
He stretched out his hand, caught hold of her.
He brought her back to him into the ark.
He waited a further seven days.
Again he sent out the dove from the ark.
The dove returned to him in the evening.
Look: a plucked-off olive leaf in her mouth.
Thus Noah knew that the waters had receded from the
    earth.
He waited another seven days.
He released the dove and she never returned to him.

In the six hundred and first year of Noah's life,
On the first month, on the first day of the month,
The waters began to be drained from the earth.
Noah removed the ark's covering.
He looked: see, the land was almost dry.
On the second month – on the twenty-seventh day –
The earth was completely dry.

God instructed Noah with these words: "Depart from the ark
You, your wife, your sons, and your sons' wives with you;
And every living creature which is with you;
All flesh, fowl, animals, everything which crawls upon the
    earth,
Bring them out with you that they may swarm over the earth,
That they may be fruitful and increase upon the earth.

Noah came out with his sons, his wife and his sons' wives;
Also, every living being, every crawling creature,
Every bird, everything which moved on the earth,
Went out from the ark, one family after another.

Noah built an altar to the LORD.
He took of all the species of clean animals
And of all the species of clean birds
He offered them as total burnt offerings upon the altar,
Not eating any of their parts but
Sacrificing them all to God.
The LORD inhaled the pleasant odour and
The LORD said in his heart:
"I will never again curse the land because of mankind
Because **I now know that**
The inclination of Man's heart **and mind**
Is evil from the time of his youth.
Never again will I destroy all life,
As I have done.
As long as the earth endures
Sowing and reaping
Cold spells and warm spells
Summer and winter
Day and night
Will not cease."

For in the image of God did he make man

God blessed Noah and his sons. He said to them,
"Be fruitful, increase and fill the earth.
The fear and dread of you shall be upon
All the living creatures on earth, all the birds of heaven,
On everything which crawls on land, all the fish of the sea.
Into your hands they are given.
Unlike the days when I created Man,
Every living creature will be yours for food.

Just as the vegetation, I have given it all for you to eat.
Only do not eat flesh while it has its life – its blood – in it.
But heed this: for the shedding of your own life's blood
I will hold every beast accountable.
Of every man too, of every man who destroys his brother's life,
I will demand the life of that man."
Whoever sheds the blood of man
For that man his blood will be shed,
For in the image of God
Did he make man.
"Now, you, be fruitful and increase,
Abound over the earth and rule over it."

God spoke again to Noah and his sons with him:
"As for me: Behold I am making a covenant
With you and your descendants after you;
And with all the living creatures with you,
The birds, the cattle, the beasts of the earth with you –
Everything that came out of the ark,
Every living creature on earth.
This is the covenant I am agreeing with you:
Never again will all flesh be cut off by flood waters.
No more will there be a flood to lay waste the earth."
God said: "This is the sign of the covenant
Which I make between you and me,
Between every living creature who is with you
Unto generations without end.
I have placed my bow into the clouds.
It is the sign between me and the earth.
When I disperse clouds over the earth,
When the bow appears amidst the clouds,
I will remember my covenant which is between
Me and you and between every living creature, all flesh:
That the waters will not become a flood to wipe out all flesh.
Yes, when the bow is in the clouds,
I will see it to remember the unending covenant

Between God and between every living creature
And all flesh upon the earth."
God repeated this to Noah, "This is the sign of
The covenant which I have made between me
And all flesh which is upon the earth."

So the sons of Noah who left the ark were
Shem, Ham and Japheth; Ham was Canaan's father.
These three were the sons of Noah,
From whom the whole earth branched out.
Now Noah was the first, being a tiller of the soil,
To plant a vineyard.
He drank of the wine and became drunk.
In his drunkenness, he uncovered himself in his tent.
Ham saw the nakedness of his father, Noah.
Instead of covering him, he ran out to tell
His two brothers who were outside the tent.
Not thinking it was a laughing matter,
Shem and Japheth took a garment,
Placed it upon both their backs,
Walked backwards into the tent,
Covered the nakedness of their father.
As their faces were turned aside,
They did not see their father's nakedness.
When Noah sobered up from his wine,
He heard how his youngest son had treated him.
He said: "Cursed be Cain, Ham's son."[1]
Let him be the lowest of slaves to his brothers.
Furthermore, he said, "Blessed be the LORD,
The God of Shem; Let Canaan be his slave.
Let God enlarge the borders of Japheth.

[1] To curse a son for a father's sin appears unjust. In the context of the author's view that a child is a mere extension of his parent, no moral problem arises over the punishment of a son because of his father. Note the Second Commandment: "I the LORD your God am a passionate God punishing the fault of the parent upon the children, grandchildren and great-grandchildren of those who reject me." [Exodus 20:5]

Let him dwell in the settlements of Shem
And let Canaan be slaves to both."
This curse was fulfilled when the descendants of Shem,
The people of Israel, conquered the land of Canaan:
In the days of Joshua they made slaves
Of the Gibeonites, the descendants of Canaan.
Noah after the flood lived for three hundred and fifty years
Thus all the days of Noah were
Nine hundred and fifty years when he died.
The descendants of Noah's sons,
Shem, Ham and Japheth, and the lands
They ruled are recorded in the Book of Genealogies.[1]

Now the whole world had only one language,
Everyone using identical words.
When they migrated from the east
They touched upon a valley in the Land of Shinar.
They settled there and said one to the other:
"Shall we not make bricks, well burnt and hard."
Bricks took the place of stone; bitumen was used for mortar.
"Now," they said, "let us build ourselves a city
With the top of its tower touching the heavens.
This will make a name for us
For the tower will be seen by everyone,
Preventing us **from losing our bearings and**
Being scattered over the face of the whole earth.

The Lord descended to look at the city and
The tower which the sons of man had built.
The Lord said, "Consider, they are one people,
All sharing one language.
If this is how they are beginning to behave
Nothing which they conspire to do
Will be beyond their reach.
Come then, let us go down,

[1] See appendix 1. For Genesis 10:2–32

Let us confuse their language
So that they will not be able to understand each
    other."
This is how the LORD scattered them from there
Over the face of the whole earth, for
Not being able to understand each other
They had to stop building the city.
This is why the place is called Babylonia
Because there the LORD babbled up
The language of man and from there
The LORD scattered them over the face of the earth.

The Ten Generations from Shem to Abraham

This is the line of Shem.
As there were ten generations from Adam to Noah,
So the generations from Noah's son to Abraham also
    number ten:
1. Shem was 100 years old when he sired Arpachshad
    Two years after the flood. After his birth he lived 500
        years.

    He sired sons and daughters, **dying at the age of 600.**
2. When Arpachshad was 35 years old, he sired Shelah.
    After his birth he lived 403 years.

    He sired sons and daughters, **dying at the age of 438.**
3. When Shelah was 30 years old, he sired Eber.
    After his birth he lived 403 years.

    He sired sons and daughters, **dying at the age of 433.**
4. When Eber, **ancestor of the Hebrews,** was 34 years,
    He sired Peleg. After his birth he lived 430 years.

    He sired sons and daughters, **dying at the age of 464.**
5. When Peleg was 30 years old, he sired Reu.
    After his birth, he lived 209 years.

    He sired sons and daughters, **dying at the age of 239.**

6. When Reu was 32 years old, he sired Serug.
   After his birth, he lived 207 years.
   He sired sons and daughter, **dying at the age of 239.**
7. When Serug was 30 years old, he sired Nahor.
   After his birth, he lived 200 years.
   He sired sons and daughters, **dying at the age of 230.**
8. When Nahor was 29 years old, he sired Terah.
   After his birth, he lived 119 years.
   He sired sons and daughters, **dying at the age of 148.**
9. When Terah had lived 70 years,
10. He sired Abram, Nahor and Haran.
    And Haran sired Lot, **Abram's nephew.**
    Haran died while his father Terah, was still alive
    In his native land, Ur of the Chaldeans.

Abram and Nahor took to themselves wives,
The name of Abram's wife was Sarai
Nahor's wife was Milcah [his niece],
The daughter of Haran, **his deceased brother**
Haran, the father of Lot,
Was also the father of Milcah and Isca.
Is it not said that Isca was Sarai?
As Nahor married Milcah, Abraham married Sarai
So that the daughters of their dead brother Haran
Should not be destitute without support.

Now, Sarai was barren; she was without child.
Terah gathered together his son Abram,
His grandson Lot ben[1] Haran,
His **granddaughter and** daughter-in-law, Sarai,
The wife of Abram, his son, and
Set out together with them from Ur of the Chaldeans
For the land of Canaan, but when

---

[1] ben means 'son of'. The English equivalent of ben Haran wold be Haranson,
like Richardson. I have not translated 'ben' whenever it occurs as 'son of' but
have kept to the Hebrew original.

They came to the land of Haran, they settled there.
The days of Terah came to 205 years;
And Terah died in Haran.

I shall make you a great nation

The LORD said to Abram, "Go from your land, yes
From your very birthplace, even from your father's house
To the land that I shall show you.
I shall make you a great nation,
I will bless you, I will make you famous.
You will be invoked as a blessing.
Those who call you blessed, I will bless;
Those who curse you, will I curse!
All the families of the earth will aspire to your blessedness."

So Abram went as the LORD had commanded him,
Lot, his nephew, went with him,
Abram was seventy-five years old
When he left Haran.
Abram took Sarai, his wife, and Lot, his brother's son,
And all the possessions they had amassed,
And all the servants they had acquired.
Off they went towards the land of Canaan.
On their arrival in Canaan, Abram passed through the land
Until he stopped at the site of Shechem,
At the place of the Oak of Oracles.
At that time the Canaanites controlled the land.

There, the LORD appeared to Abram and promised him:
"To your descendants will I give this land."
At that place, he built an altar
To the LORD who appeared to him.
From there he moved on to the hill country east of Bethel
He pitched camp between Bethel on the west and
Ai on the east.
There too he built an altar to the LORD,

And invoked him by the name of the LORD.
Then Abram journeyed gradually southwards to the Negev.

When the land suffered from famine,
Abram went down to Egypt
To stay there for a time because the
Famine was so severe in Canaan.
As he came near to entering Egypt, he said to Sarai, his wife:
"I have always known that you are an attractive woman.
It could be that when the Egyptians see you and say
'She is his wife', they will kill me but keep you alive.
Please, tell them that you are my sister,
So that I may be favoured because of you,
And my life will be spared for your sake."

When Abram entered Egypt,
The Egyptians stared at the woman,
Because she was very beautiful.
The courtiers of Pharaoh saw her,
And raved about her to Pharaoh;
Thus the woman was taken to the Pharaoh's palace.
As for Abram, he prospered because of her.
He was given sheep, oxen, asses, male and female slaves,
She-asses and camels.

But the LORD struck Pharaoh with horrendous plagues,
Also his household on account of Sarai, Abram's wife.
Pharaoh made enquiries and discovered the truth.
Pharaoh summoned Abram: "What is this
That you have done to me?
Why did you not tell me that she was your wife?
Why did you say: 'She is my sister', so I took her as my wife?
Here is your wife, take her and good riddance to you."
Pharaoh gave new orders regarding him.
So they expelled him and his wife and all his company.

So Abram went up from Egypt towards the Negev,
He, his wife, his entire company, and Lot's household.

Now, Abram's wealth was very substantial:
Cattle, silver and gold.
He journeyed by stages from the Negev to Bethel,
Where he first established his camp between Bethel and Ai.
To the place of the altar he built
When he first came to Canaan.
There Abram invoked the name of the LORD.

Lot, who accompanied Abram, also had flocks, herds and tents.
The land was not large enough to allow them to live together,
Because their possessions were so great,
It was not possible for them to share one settlement.
The shepherds of Abram and the shepherds of Lot quarrelled.
They were competing for pasture land and water for
The Canaanites and the Perizzites were still in the land.

Abram said to Lot: "Let there be no friction between
Me and you, between my shepherds and yours,
For we are kinsmen. Is not the whole land before you?
Please, separate your company from mine.
If you decide to go to the left,
I will make to the right, but
If you choose the right, to the left will I go."
Lot cast his eyes around, and saw that
The Jordan Plains were well watered [that is
Before the LORD's destruction of Sodom and Gomorrah].
It was like the LORD's garden, **as fertile** as the land of Egypt,
The lushness you see as you approach Zoar.
So Lot, for his part, chose all of the Jordan Plains,
And he journeyed eastwards.
So the kinsmen put a distance between themselves.

Abram settled in the land of Canaan and
Lot made his camp in the cities of the Plain
And pitched his tents up to Sodom.
The men of Sodom were wicked and were constantly
Sinning against the LORD.

But the LORD said to Abram after Lot separated from him:
"Look around and know that from the place you stand,
Notwithstanding your undertaking to Lot,
The north, southwards to the Negev,
East, westwards to the sea,
All the land which you can see I will give to you,
To your descendants as long as the world lasts.
I will make your descendants like the dust of the earth –
If a man can count the dust of the earth
He will also be able to count your descendants.
Rise up, traverse the land,
Its entire breadth and width,
Because I have given it to you."
Abram pitched his tents here and there,
Until he came to settle by the oaks of Mamre,
Which are in Hebron; there he built an altar to the LORD.

It was in the days of **the four great kings:**
    Hammurabi, king of Babylonia
    Eriagu, king of Larsa
    Chedorlaomer, king of Elam, and
    Tidal, king of the 'hordes' of the north.

They did battle against **the five kings of the Plains:**
    'Evil', king of Sodom
    'Wickedness', king of Gomorrah
    Shinab, king of Admah
    Shemeber, king of Zeboiim,
    The king of Bela, known as Zoar.

All these kings mustered together to do battle
In the Valley of Siddin, that is the Salt Sea.
Before this battle, they, **the five kings,** were vassals to
Chedorlaomer, **king of Elam.**
In the thirteenth year, they rebelled.
In the fourteenth year, Chedorlaomer and
The kings who sallied forth with him campaigned and

Defeated the giants of Rephaim at the
Battle of the Rams of Ashteroth; also the
Giants of Zamzummim at the battle on the Plain of Kiriathaim.
And the Horites in the mountains of Seir,
As far as the Terebinth of Paran, by the wilderness.

Elated by their great victories, they returned and forayed into
The Spring of Justice, that is Kadesh, and smote
The entire domain of the Amalekites,
And also the Amorites who lived in Hazazon-tamar.
Knowing that they would be next in line of their
   onslaught,
   The king of Sodom,
   The king of Gomorrah,
   The king of Admah,
   The king of Zeboiim.
   The king of Bela, that is Zoar,
Decided on a pre-emptive strike.
They mustered against them
To do battle in the Valley of Siddim, against
   Chedorlaomer, king of Elam
   Tidal, king of the hordes of the north
   Hammurabi, king of Babylonia
   Eriagu, king of Larsa
Four kings against five.

Now the valley of Siddim was full of slime pits.
The kings of the Plains of the Jordan
Could not withstand the forces of their enemies.
The kings of Sodom and Gomorrah fled, and
Their troops fell there **in the slime pits**.
The others that survived fled to the mountains.
They, **the armies of the four kings,**
Took all the goods of Sodom and Gomorrah,
And all their grain and went off triumphantly.
They took Lot, Abram's brother's son who lived in Sodom,
His goods, and they departed triumphantly.

One who escaped came and told Abram, the Hebrew,
Who was then dwelling in the field of oak trees
Belonging to Mamre, the Amorite, the brother of
Eshkol and the brother of Aner.
Now, they had made an alliance with Abram.
When Abram heard that his kinsman was taken captive,
He drew out his best men, those born in his house,
Numbering three hundred and eighteen; they **and**
The forces of his allies went after **the four kings**
As far as the region of Dan.
They crept upon their camps by night.
Quietly, he, Abram, split his warriors into bands
Against them that night. **They were taken by surprise**
And Abram's armies smote them and chased them
As far as Hobah, which is to the left of Damascus.
He retrieved all the goods, even Lot, his kinsman,
And his possessions, he brought back –
Even all the women and the entire people.

The king of Sodom, **who had escaped,** welcomed him
After his return from defeating Chedorlaomer,
And the kings who were with him, at the
Valley of Shaveh, which is now called the King's Valley.
Melchizedek, king of Jerusalem also greeted him.
He brought out bread and wine.
He was a priest of El Elyon, God Most-High.
He blessed him saying: "Blessed be Abram of
God Most-High, author of heaven and earth.
And blessed be God Most-High who
Delivered your enemies into your hands."
He, gave him a tenth of all the booty.
The king of Sodom said: "Just give me my people –
You can keep the property."
But Abram said to the king of Sodom:
"I lift up my hand to the Lord, to God Most-High.
I swear, not a thread, not a thong of a sandal

Will I take, so that you will not say,
'It was I who made Abram rich.'
Nothing except what the lads have eaten,
And a portion of the spoils for the men who joined me.
Let Aner, Eshkol and Mamre take their share."

After these events, **some thirteen years later**,
The voice of the Lord came to Abram in a vision:
"Never fear, Abram, I am your shield,
Your reward will be very great."
Abram said, "Lord, my master,
What can you give me **of any worth**,
Seeing that I am **going to die** childless.
Eliezer, the chief bailiff will be like my son."
Abram continued: "Look, you have given me no children,
So a member of my staff will inherit my estate."
But, the voice of the Lord came to him saying,
"This man will not be your heir,
Only the one who comes out of your loins,
He will be your heir."

He instructed him to go outside.
He said to him, "Look towards the heavens,
And count the stars; can you count them?
So great will be the number of your descendants."
He had trust in the Lord,
Who considered this to be to his credit.
He said to him: "I am the Lord,
Who took you out of Ur of the Chaldeans
To give you this land to inherit."
He replied, "Lord, my master,
How can I be sure that I will inherit it?"

He said to him, **"I will enter into a covenant with you.
And what I now instruct you to do
Will be the form of the contract between us.**
Bring me a heifer who is three years old;

Also, a three-year-old she-goat;
A three-year-old ram, a turtle dove and young bird."
He took all these creatures.
He split them down the middle
And placed each half opposite the other,
Except for the bird which he did not divide into two.
When the birds of prey descended upon the slain animals,
Abram drove them off. As the sun was going down,
A deep sleep overtook Abram in which
A fearsome and great darkness enveloped him.
He heard the voice of the Lord saying to Abram,
"Know for certain that your descendants will be
Aliens in a land not theirs.
They shall be enslaved and oppressed for four hundred years.
But fear not, for over the nation who enslaves them, I will
Execute judgement; they will leave with great wealth,
As you once did when you left Egypt.
But you will not suffer to witness this.
You will go down to your ancestors peacefully.
You will be buried at a ripe old age.
The fourth[1] generation will come back here
For the Amorites have not yet sufficiently sinned
To justify my giving their land to your descendants."
When the sun had gone fully down and it was dark,
There appeared a smoking firebrand and a
Flaming torch which passed between
Those **divided** parts **of the animals.**
On that **very** day, the Lord 'cut' a covenant with Abram,
By passing between the divided animal pieces, saying:
"To your descendants will I give this land
From the river of Egypt to the great river, the Euphrates –
The land of the Kenites, the Kenizzites, the Kadmonites,

---

[1] As God earlier advises Abraham of four hundred years of oppression, the author appears to consider, at least in this context, a generation to be a hundred years.

The Hittites, the Perizzites, the Rephaites, the Amorites,
The Canaanites, the Girgarshites and the Jebusites."

Do with her what you will

Sarai, the wife of Abram, did not bear children for him.
She had a handmaiden from Egypt, named Hagar.
Sarai said to Abram, "Seeing that the Lord
Has prevented me from bearing, go into my handmaiden.
Perhaps, I will have a son through her."
And Abram agreed to Sarai's proposal.
Now, Sarai, the wife of Abram, had taken Hagar the Egyptian,
To be her handmaiden ten years after
Abram had settled in the land of Canaan.
She gave her to Abram her husband to be his wife.
He slept with Hagar and she conceived.
When she saw that she was pregnant,
She became disdainful of her mistress.
So Sarai complained to Abram,
"I have been wronged because of you.
It was I who put my handmaiden into your arms,
And now that she is pregnant
I am held in contempt by her.
Why did you not keep her in her place?
Let the Lord judge between me and you!"
Abram **brushed her aside and** said to Sarai,
"**I have done nothing wrong.
As you said, it was your doing**.
Your handmaiden is under your control
Do with her what you will!"
So Sarai persecuted her so that she fled from her.
And a Messenger of the Lord found her by
A spring of water in the wilderness,
The spring on the way to Shur.
He said: "Hagar! O handmaiden of Sarai
 Whence have you come and

Whither do you go?"
She answered: "Before Sarai, my mistress, I am fleeing."
The Messenger of the LORD said to her:

"Return to your mistress and
Endure her oppressive hand."

Moreover, the Messenger of the LORD said to her:

"I will so greatly increase your descendants
None will be able to count their great number."

The Messenger of the LORD said to her:

"You are with child
You shall bear a son.
You shall name him Ishmael [God hears]
Because the Lord has heard of your oppression.
He will be a wild ass of a man,
His hand against every man, and
Every man's hand striking against him.
He shall have no settled place but
He shall live among his kinsmen."

She called the LORD's name who had spoken to her,
"You are my seeing God", because she thought,
"I saw **him** even after he saw me."
Therefore that spring was called the Spring of
'The Living One who Sees Me'.
It is between Kadesh and Bered.

Hagar bore a son to Abram and
Abram called the name of his son
Whom Hagar bore for him Ishmael.
Abram was eighty-six years old
When Hagar gave birth to Ishmael for Abram.

Kings will come out of you

Abram was ninety-nine years old when
The Lord appeared to Abram, when he said to him:
  "I am 'God Shaddai'[1]
  Walk before me
  Strive to be perfect!
  I will establish my covenant between me and you
  I will make your numbers exceedingly great."
Abram prostrated himself on his face.
God continued speaking to him, saying:
"As for me, my covenant with you is this:
You will be the patriarch of a multitude of nations.
No longer will you be called by the name: Abram.
Your name will be enlarged to Abraham
Because I have made you the
Patriarch of a multitude of nations.
I will make you exceedingly fruitful
I will make nations of you and
Kings will come out of you.
I will establish my covenant between me and you
And between your descendants after you
For generations **and generations** –
A covenant without end.
To be God to you
And to your descendants after you.
I will give to you the land where you have sojourned.
That is all the land of Canaan for an eternal inheritance.
I will be God to them." God continued speaking to Abraham,
"As for you, keep **your part of** my covenant,
You, your descendants after you for all their generations.

This **is the sign of** my covenant which you must keep
Between me and you and your descendants after you:

---

[1] Normally, translated: Almighty God, but there is no linguistic reason for
doing so.

Genesis 17:10–18

Circumcise every male among you!
You shall circumcise the flesh of the foreskin.
This will be the sign of the covenant between me and you.
At the age of eight days, shall every male be circumcised
Among you throughout your generations.
All – the homeborn servants, those purchased with money
From whoever, even though they are not your children.
They shall certainly be circumcised,
Homeborn servants or purchased with silver.
Thus my covenant will be a mark in your flesh
As an eternal covenant.
And if any uncircumcised male does not
Circumcise the flesh of his foreskin,
That person shall be cut off from his people.
He has broken my covenant!"

Let Ishmael live in your favour[1]

And God said to Abraham, "As for your wife Sarai,
She is part of my covenant with you.
I will enlarge her name.
No longer shall you call her Sarai, but Sarah is her name.
I will bless her too: even give you a son by her.
I will bless her. She will be the mother of nations,
Kings of peoples will issue from her womb."
Abraham prostrated himself face down on the earth,
But he laughed, saying to himself,
"Can a child be born to a man who is a hundred years old?
Will Sarah who is ninety years old give birth?"
But what Abraham said to God was,
"I would be happy if Ishmael were to be my heir.
Let Ishmael live in your favour!"

[1] What follows are two different accounts of the birth of Isaac, one in which Abraham laughs and the other in which Sarah laughs. Both explain why their son is named "Laughter".

34

But God insisted: "*No*, Sarah your wife will bear you a son.
You will name him Isaac **because I heard you laugh.**
With him will I establish my covenant and
An eternal covenant with his descendants after him.
As for your son Ishmael, I have heard your petition.
See, I have blessed him!
I will make him very fruitful and very numerous.
He will father twelve princes; I will make him a great nation.
But my special covenant I establish with Isaac whom Sarah
Will bear to you, at this season next year."
He finished speaking to him, stood up and left Abraham.
Abraham took Ishmael, his son, and all his homeborn servants,
The men he bought with silver –
All the men of Abraham's camp.
He circumcised the flesh of their foreskins,
On the day that God spoke to him.
As we said: Abraham was ninety-nine years old
When the flesh of his foreskin was circumcised,
And Ishmael his son was thirteen years old,[1]
When the flesh of his foreskin was circumcised.
On that day Abraham and Ishmael were circumcised,
And all his household, his homeborn servants,
Those bought with money were circumcised.

At another time the LORD appeared to him
When he lived by the oaks of Mamre,
While he was sitting by the entrance to his tents.
It was the hottest part of the day.
This is the way the Lord appeared to him:
He looked up and three men were looming over him.
He ran from the entrance of his tents to greet them.
He bowed to the ground. "My lords,
If I have found favour with you,
Please do not pass by your servant.

---

[1] This might be an indication that circumcision was originally an ordeal
endured at puberty as proof of manhood.

Let some water be fetched; bathe your feet and rest by the tree.
I will fetch some food to refresh yourselves;
Then go on your way.
Surely, it is not by chance
You come this way to your servant."
They replied: "Excellent, do as you propose."
Abraham dashed into the tents to find Sarah,
"Be quick, take three large measures of choice flour,
Knead and make loaves of bread."
He then ran to the herd, picked a tender and choice yearling,
Gave it to a lad who hastened to prepare it, fetched
Curds, milk and the cooked yearling to put before them.
He remained standing in attendance upon them
Under the tree while they ate.
Then, they asked him: "Now where is Sarah your wife?"
Surely, they must be men of the Lord,
For how else could they have known her name?
He replied: "She is there in the tent."
One of them said, "I shall return to you in the spring,
Be assured that Sarah your wife will have a son."
Sarah was listening at the entrance of the camp behind him.
Now Abraham and Sarah were old, advanced in years.
Sarah had stopped menstruating, so Sarah laughed to herself,
Thinking, "After I am dried up,
Shall I have delights when my husband is also old.
The LORD, **one of the three men**, questioned Abraham,
"Now, why then has Sarah laughed, saying,
'Is it possible that I will give birth being so old?'
(Discreetly holding back
What Sarah said about Abraham's age.)
Is there anything too wonderful for the LORD to perform!
I will return next year at springtime.
Sarah will have a son." Sarah defended herself,
"I did not laugh," because she was in such a fright.
He would not accept this: "Not so; You did laugh!"

Will the Judge of the whole earth . . . ?

Two of the men set off to go towards Sodom.
Abraham went with them to see them off.
The LORD **remained behind for he** thought,
"Shall I hide from Abraham what I am going to do?
Seeing that Abraham will become a great and powerful nation,
All the peoples of the earth will wish to be blessed as he.
For I have made myself known to him,
So that he might instruct his children and his house
Who come after him to keep the ways of the LORD,
To act with righteousness and justice so that the LORD can
Deliver the promises made to him.
 For the LORD had thought:
"The outcry of **the oppressed in**
Sodom and Gomorrah is very great.
Their sinfulness has become too serious to endure.
I will go down and see whether their actions are in keeping
With the outcries which have reached me;
If they are not so great, I will know."
He had gone down and their sinfulness was very great.
So two of the Men went from there to Sodom
To save Lot and his family from destruction.
But Abraham was still standing before the LORD.
When the Lord told him, Abraham approached and asked:
"Will you really destroy the righteous with the wicked?
Let us say that there were fifty righteous men in the city,
Would you destroy it? Would you not spare the place,
For the sake of the fifty righteous men in it?
It would not be proper for you to do such a thing –
To kill the righteous with the wicked, so that there is
No difference between the fate of the righteous and the wicked.
It would be improper for you!
Will the Judge of the whole earth not act with justice?"
The Lord was pleased that Abraham challenged him.
The LORD said, "If I find in Sodom fifty righteous men

In the city, I will spare the place for their sake.
Abraham responded, "See, I have begun to speak to the LORD,
I who am but dust and ashes, **but as I have begun . . .**
Suppose of the fifty righteous five were missing.
For the missing five would you destroy the whole city?"
God smiled at Abraham's bargaining. "Do not talk about five!
I agree not to destroy the city if I find forty-five."
Abraham persisted in pleading with him,
"Suppose forty were found there?"
He agreed: "I will not do it for the sake of the forty."
"Please let me not anger my LORD so that
I may continue to speak: Suppose thirty were found there?"
– "I will not do it if I find thirty."
– "As I have had the audacity to speak to the LORD
Perhaps twenty could be found there?"
– "I will not destroy for the sake of the twenty."
– "Please, do not let my Lord be angry, and
I will speak for the last time.
Suppose ten were found there?"
– "I will not destroy for the sake of the ten."
God thought: "I chose well in choosing Abraham.
When I told Noah of the destruction of the world,
He saved himself and his family but never pleaded for others.
But there are not even ten righteous in the city of Sodom."
The LORD went away after he finished speaking to Abraham.
Abraham also returned to his own place.

The two Messengers of God arrived at Sodom in the evening.
Lot, **an elder of the city**, was sitting by the gates of Sodom.
When Lot saw them, **he knew that these were men of God.**
He stood up to greet them, bowed with his face to the ground,
"Please my lords, turn in, my lords, to your servant's home.
Lodge there after rinsing your feet.
Rise as early as you like and go on your way."
They replied: "No, we can lie down in the street."
He put great pressure on them to listen to him

So they turned to go with him and entered his house.
He prepared a feast for them,
Baked unleavened bread, and they ate.
Before they went to sleep, men of the town, natives of Sodom,
Surrounded the house, young and old –
Almost the entire people.
They were screaming at Lot:
"Where are the men who came to you tonight?
Send them out to us so that we might lie with them."
Lot thought, "There will be no stopping their wickedness!
I must show them the evil of their ways.
They know how much I love my daughters;
That I have not married them to the evil young men.
When I offer them my daughters, they will know
How even more sinful it is to violate innocent strangers."
Lot went out to them, closing the door behind him.
He pleaded, "Please, my brothers, do not do this wrong.
Look, I have two daughters who are virgins.
I will send them out to you and do with them as you see fit.
Only do not hurt these men, for they came.
To enjoy the protection of my roof."
"Stand back," they retorted: They then spoke **with contempt:**
"Look at this one, **a stranger who** comes to settle with us.
Now he wants to be a judge over us.
In that case, we will treat you worse than them."
Then they pushed hard against the man, against Lot,
They moved to break down the door.
The Men from the LORD stretched out their hands and pulled
Lot into the house and closed the door.
The people who were at the door of the house,
Young and old –
They were struck with a blinding light.
They were not able to find the door.
The Men from the LORD asked Lot,
"Who else do you have here?
Sons-in-law, your sons and your daughters –

Everything that is yours in the city, get them out of here!
Because we are destroying this place since the outcry
Against them before the LORD is so great,
The LORD sent us here to destroy it."
So Lot went to speak to the men engaged to his daughters,
"Get up, leave this place because
The LORD is to destroy the city."
But his future sons-in-law thought he was joking.

And she became a pillar of salt

At the stroke of dawn, the two Messengers urged Lot,
"Up, take your wife and the two daughters who are here,
Lest you be consumed because of the sinfulness of the city."
They delayed, **confused as to what to take with them.**
The Men, **anxious for his safety,** grabbed him by the hand,
Also the hand of his wife and the hands of his two daughters.
For the LORD took mercy upon him and his family.
So he and his family were taken outside the city.
He said, "Run for your lives, do not look behind you.
Do not think of your possessions you leave behind.
Do not stop anywhere in the plain, but run for the hills.
Otherwise, you will be consumed."
But Lot pleaded with them, "My Lords, please do not press me!
As your servant has already enjoyed your favour,
Show me now even greater kindness
Than you have already done.
You have indeed saved my life, but I am not able
To escape to the hills where other evils may overtake me;
I may die. There is a small village nearby to which I can flee.
Is it not tiny? **Show it mercy that my life**
May be saved by going there."
He replied, "I will show favour to you also in this matter.
I will not overturn the village you mention.
Now, hurry, escape there, for I will not be able to do anything
Until you arrive." Thus, the village was called Zoar [tiny].

The sun had come over the earth when Lot reached Zoar.
Then the LORD rained upon Sodom and Gomorrah
Brimstone and fire. From the LORD it came out of the sky.
Thus, he overwhelmed those cities and the entire plain,
And all the inhabitants of the cities,
Even everything which grew out of the ground.
As they entered Zoar, his wife looked back and
She became a pillar of salt,
For disobeying the Messengers of the Lord.

Abraham got up early in the morning, to go to the place
Where he stood in the presence of the LORD.
He looked towards Sodom and Gomorrah
And towards the whole plain and
He saw smoke ascending from the land
Like the smoke of a burning furnace.
So it was, when God destroyed the cities of the Plain
God remembered his covenant with Abraham, and
Sent out Lot, his nephew, out of the destruction
When he overturned the cities in which Lot had dwelt.

There is no man to lie with us

Lot left Zoar, to live in the hills with his two daughters.
He was frightened of staying in Zoar
Because the burning and the smoke were so close.
He and his two daughters made a cave their home.
Lot, stunned by grief, did not speak to his daughters,
They thought that only they had escaped.
The elder said to the younger, "Our father is old.
There is no man in the land to lie with us
As is the way of the earth to create life.
Come, we will make our father drunk with wine.
We will lie down with him and from our father's loins
We will give life to his descendants."
That night they plied him with wine and

The firstborn came in and lay with her father.
He was not aware of her lying down nor her rising up.
On the next day, the elder said to the younger,
"See, yesterday I lay with my father.
We will ply him also this night with wine.
Then go in and lie with him, that from our father
We will give life to his descendants."
Thus, they plied their father with wine also that night.
The younger went up to him and lay with him.
He was not aware of her lying down nor her rising up.
Thus were the two daughters of Lot pregnant by their father.
The firstborn gave birth to a son.
She named him Moab –
He is the ancestor of the Moabites of our time.
The younger also gave birth to a son.
She named him Ben Ammi[1] –
He is the ancestor of the Ammonites of our time.
Is this not why – when the children of Israel left Egypt and
Neither the nations of Moab and Amnon allowed them to pass
Through their borders – that it was decreed
Their descendants would never enter the community of Israel?
It is the Law that those borne to women
Out of their fathers' loins
May never join the House of Israel
Nor enter the Lord's sanctuary,
Their ancestors were bastards by birth.
And they were pariahs by what they did to their kinsmen
By not permitting them to journey through their land
When they made their way to the land which
The Lord their God had promised to give them.[2]

[1] Moab's Hebrew meaning is "from father" and similarly the meaning of Ben
Ammi is "son of my people".
[2] No doubt, an Israelite slander against the nations of Moab and Amnon
because of the enmity between them and Israel. The first indication of this was
their refusal, according to later biblical account, to allow them to pass through
their territories on the way to the promised land

How have I sinned against you

And the Lord restored Sarah's youth.
Indeed, she was fair to look upon and
Again she knew the ways of women.
The Lord also restored the virility of Abraham.
He took delight in Sarah and they lay together
And waited for the Lord's promise to be fulfilled,
That a son would be born to them.

Abraham journeyed from there, **the Oaks of Mamre,**
Towards the south country, the Negev, and settled between
Kadesh and Shure. He lived in Gerar, **a city of Philistia.**
Fearing that Sarah's beauty would endanger his life,
He said about Sarah: "She is my sister."
Abimelech, king of Gerar sent his men and took Sarah.
But God caused a heavy weariness to come over Abimelech
So that he went to his bed and slept.
God appeared to Abimelech in a dream that very night.
He said to him. "You are a dead man because of
The woman whom you seized for she is a married woman."
Now, Abimelech had not yet approached her sexually.
He objected, "My Lord, will you even destroy
A nation of the righteous: he said to me: 'She is my sister.'
She also said: 'He is my brother.'
With proper intentions and pure hands did I do this."
God replied to him in the dream, "Yes, though you took her
I was aware that you did it with honest intentions.
So I restrained you, **in your lust**, from sinning against me.
Therefore, it was I who did not allow you to touch her.
Now, send back the man's wife for he is my oracle,[1]
Let him pray on your behalf so that you may live.
If you do not return her **and persuade him to pray for you,**

---

[1] While Abraham is in the wrong, he is still God's chosen and therefore, in spite of his imperfection, under God's protection. This would no longer be an acceptable concept.

Know that your death is a certainty,
You and everyone that is yours."

Abimelech woke up in the morning and
Summoned his ministers,
To tell them in confidence all that had happened.
The men were very worried.
Abimelech summoned Abraham and questioned him:
"What have you done to us?
How have I sinned against you?
That you should bring upon me
And my kingdom a great sin!
Deeds which should not be done,
You have committed against me!"
Abimelech took breath and again spoke to Abraham:
"What did you experience here that
Made you do such a thing?"
Abraham replied: "I thought, there is no fear of God here
And that they would kill me because of my wife.
I did not really lie, for in truth, it can be said that
She is my sister, for she is the daughter of Haran,
My deceased half-brother. When he died
My father adopted his children, Lot, Milcah and Sarah
To be his own son and daughters.
He gave Milcah to my brother Nahor as a wife.
To me he gave Sarah as a wife.
She is the daughter of my father, and so my sister
And also my wife, but not the daughter of my mother.
When it happened that God led me from my father's house,
Seeing how beautiful she was, I said to her,
"Do this kindness for me; in every place to which
We shall come, say of me: 'He is my brother.'"
Abimelech was angered by the words of Abraham;
For Abraham had acted with deceit against him.
He remembered his dream, what God said to him.
He needed Abraham's prayers if he was to live.

44

Abimelech took sheep and cattle, male and female slaves,
And gave them to Abraham when he returned to him
Sarah, his wife. Abimelech also said to him,
"Look, the land is before you, settle where you please."
To Sarah he said **with bitterness**,
"Look, I have given a thousand pieces of silver
To your **so-called** brother. Let him continue to be
Your cover and for all who are with you.
Just let me be." Sarah felt **ashamed and** admonished.
Abraham prayed to God and he healed Abimelech,
His wife and concubines and they bore children.
For the LORD had **made Abimelech sterile and thus**
Closed up all the wombs in Abimelech's household
Because of what happened to Sarah, Abraham's wife.[1]

Cast out this slave woman

The LORD remembered Sarah as he had promised.
The LORD performed exactly as he had spoken.
Sarah conceived and gave birth for Abraham
A son in his advanced years
At the season which God had specified to him.
Abraham called the name of his son born to him –
Whom Sarah had borne to him – Isaac.
Abraham circumcised Isaac, his son,
When he was eight days old,
As God had commanded him.
Now, Abraham was one hundred years old
When Isaac, his son, was born to him.

---

[1] The interpretation interpolated here is that Sarah is Isca daughter of the deceased Haran, who was adopted by Terah, Abraham's father. Sarah is therefore, by his father's adoption, his sister as well as his niece. Also, the portrayal of Abraham as a deceiver under God's protection would not have disturbed the readers and listeners of this tale. They would have greatly enjoyed the saga of their patriarch's enrichment by his deception of a Philistine king and with the help of the Israelite God.

Sarah said, "God has given me a cause for laughter.
Everyone who hears of it will laugh [Yitzhak][1] with me."
For she thought, "Who would have said of Abraham
That Sarah would give suck to children?
For I have borne him a son in his old age."
The boy grew up and was weaned.
Abraham made a great feast on the day of Isaac's weaning.
When Sarah saw the son of Hagar teasing Isaac,
She said to Abraham, "Cast out this slave woman
And her son, because the son of this slave woman
Will not inherit with my son Isaac.
She will go away as she came – with nothing."
This was very displeasing to Abraham
Because of his love for his son. God said to Abraham,
"Be not distraught over the lad and your slave woman.
Do whatever Sarah your wife has requested of you."
Abraham protested, "Let me send them away then, but
With silver, and male and female servants
For he too is my son, indeed my first born."
God replied, "No, obey her voice. It is I who will bless him.
But, you shall be known because of the descendants of Isaac.
I will also make of the son of this slave woman a nation.
He will be the father of twelve princes."
Abraham rose early in the morning,
Woke up Hagar and Ishmael and said, "You must go
But fear not, the Lord my God will protect you,
And make of Ishmael our son a great nation.
I cannot give you anything but this assurance."
He took food and a skin of water
He gave them to Hagar, putting them on her shoulder
Together with the lad, and sent her away.
She departed and wandered in the wilderness of Beersheba.
When there was no more water in the skin,
She put the child down under one of the bushes.

---

[1] "Yitzhak" the Hebrew name of Isaac.

She left and sat down within view of him,
At a distance about a bow shot away, for she thought,
"I do not want to see the boy die." So, sitting opposite him,
She raised her voice and began to wail.
God had heard the moaning of the lad.
A Messenger of God cried out to Hagar,
"What troubles you, Hagar? Do not be afraid.
For God has heard the cry of the lad.
Stand up, carry the lad and hold him by the hand
Because I am going to make him into a great nation."
God opened her eyes so that she saw a well of water.
She went there and filled the skin with water.
She quenched the thirst of the lad. So it was that
God was with the lad and he grew up to adulthood.
He settled in the wilderness of Paran and became an archer.
His mother got him a wife from the land of Egypt.

At that time, Abimelech, also Phicol[1], the chief of his troops,
Said to Abraham, "We know that God is with you in all you do,
Now swear to me by God, here and now,
That you will not deal falsely with me
Nor with my son nor with my grandson after me
And with the people of the land in which you sojourn."
Be as kind to me as I have been to you.
Abraham answered, "I do so swear."
Abraham, however, did first accuse Abimelech
Over the robbery of a certain well
Committed by the servants of Abimelech. Hearing this,
Abimelech protested, "I had no inkling; who did such a thing?
You, for your part, never told me,
I, for my part, only hear of it now."
Abraham accepted Abimelech's explanations
In recognition of Abimelech's rule over the land,

---

[1] Literal meaning of Phicol is "mouth of all". He is a symbolic character who is intended by the author to represent the worries of the entire population over the threat posed to them by God's favourite, Abraham.

Abraham fetched flocks and cattle and gave them to him.
Thus with this gift they made a pact between them.
Of the flocks he had given him, Abraham set apart seven ewes.
Abimelech asked him, "Why have you separated these ewes?"
"Because," he replied, "you will take these ewes from me,
As proof of your acceptance that it was I who dug this well."
It is for this reason that this place is named Beersheba[1]
Because there the two of them swore an oath.
So they made a pact at Beersheba.
Abimelech proceeded – also Phicol, chief of his troops –
To make their way back to the land of the Philistines.
Thus did Abraham establish the right to live in the land
To dig water wells to water their flocks.
So Abraham gave thanks to the Lord for his goodness.
To give shelter to his descendants after him,
Abraham planted a tamarisk at Beersheba.
He invoked there the name of the LORD, 'Deity Eternal'.
Abraham lived in Philistia for many years.

Offer him here as a burnt offering

Abraham prospered in the land.
He was respected and his fame spread far.
God had given him a son in his old age
Who would be the father of nations, his eternal legacy.
The supreme God tested Abraham, saying to him,
"Abraham." And Abraham answered,
"Here am I." He said,
"Take your son,
Your only one,
The one you love,

---

[1] Hebrew meaning: "Oath Well" The naming of Beersheba will later also be
credited to Isaac, his son.

Isaac.
Get you to the land of Moriah.
Offer him there as a burnt offering
On one of the hills I will tell you."
Abraham thought: "The Lord promised me,
'With Isaac will I establish my covenant –
An eternal covenant with his descendants after him.'"
But Abraham kept silent.

Abraham rose early in the morning,
He saddled his donkey.
He took two of his young men with him,
And Isaac his son.
He chopped wood for the burnt offering
And prepared to go to the place
To which God would direct him.

On the third day of their journey
Abraham looked up.
He saw the appointed place at a distance.
Abraham said to his young men,
"Stay here with the donkey
I and the boy will go from here.
We will worship and return to you."

Abraham took the wood for the burnt offering,
Placed them on Isaac his son.
In his own hands he carried
The flint for the fire and the knife.
The two walked on together.

Isaac said to Abraham, his father.
He said, "My father." He answered,
"Here am I, my son, ask."
He asked, "Here is the fire and the wood,
But where is the lamb for the burnt offering?"
Abraham replied, "God will see to the lamb
For the burnt offering, my son."

And the two walked on together.

They came to the place,
Which the supreme God had appointed for him.
Abraham built an altar there.
He arranged the wood.
He bound his son Isaac
And placed him on the altar
On top of the wood.

Abraham stretched out his hand.
He took the knife
To slay his son.
A Messenger of the LORD called out to him from heaven,
He said, "Abraham, Abraham."
He replied, "Here am I."
He said, "Do not stretch out your hand against the lad;
Do not do anything to him!
For now I know
That you are in awe of God,
In that you did not hold back
Your son,
Your only one
From me."

Abraham looked up.
He saw a ram caught by its horns in a bush.
Abraham went and took the ram.
He offered it as a burnt offering
In place of his son.

Abraham called the name of that place,
"The LORD will see to it."
As it is said to this very day,
"On the mountain of the LORD, the sacrifice will appear."

And the Messenger of the LORD called Abraham
A second time from heaven:

"By my own self, I swear –
An oracle from the LORD,
Because you have acted this way,
In not holding back
Your son,
Your only one,
I will give you unending blessings.
I will make your descendants
As plentiful as the stars of the heaven
And the grains of sand on the seashore.
Your descendants will inherit
The gates of their enemies.
All nations of the earth
Will ask to be blessed like your descendants
Because you heard my voice
And obeyed my command."[1]

Abraham returned to his servants
They set off together to Beersheba
And Abraham settled there.

I will find a wife for Isaac

**Abraham thought: "I must find a wife for Isaac
But he will not take to wife a Canaanite woman."**
After this, Abraham was given interesting news:
Milcah, your niece, has borne sons to your brother Nahor.
Uz, the eldest, his brother Buz,
Kemuel, ancestor of Aram, Chesed, Hazo, Pildash, Jidlaph,
Bethuel. He sired Rebecca.

---

[1] This horrifically majestic tale demands but defies explanation. God promises
Abraham that from Isaac He will give him a great nation, then orders him to
sacrifice him The reader must be left to his imaginative devices in dealing with
it. My interpretation is to read it as a parable for the Israelites, who must have
the faith of Abraham in God who demands of them self-sacrifice for his own
sanctification, even when he does not keep his promises to deliver his people
from their enemies in spite of his covenant with them.

These were the eight sons Milcah gave to,
Abraham's brother, Nahor,
He also had a concubine named Reumah
She too had sons: Tebah, Gaham, Tahash and Maacah.
So Nahor, Abraham's brother, had twelve sons.
Abraham thought:
"In my brother's home, I will find a wife for Isaac."
Sarah lived a hundred and twenty-seven years.
This was the length of Sarah's life.
Sarah died in Kiryat-Arba – Hebron – in the land of Canaan.
Abraham began to mourn and weep over her.
Abraham left the side of his dead wife to speak to the Hittites.
He said, "I am a foreigner residing with you.
Give me a burial site so that I may bury my dead."

The Hittites replied to Abraham, saying to him,
"Listen to us, my lord, you are a prince of God in our midst.
In the choicest of our crypts, bury your dead.
Not one of us would withhold his crypts
From you to bury your dead."

Abraham stood up and bowed down low
To the elders of the people of the land, that is the Hittites.
He spoke to them these words: "If you are so inclined
To allow me to bury my dead who is before me,
Hear me and speak on my behalf to Ephron ben Zoar.[1]
Let him sell me the Cave of Machpelah, which he owns,
Which borders on his fields.
Let him sell it to me for its proper price
In your presence to be my permanent burial site."

Now Ephron was sitting among the elders of the Hittites.
Ephron, the Hittite, answered Abraham before the Hittites,
Before all who came by the gates of his city,
"No, my lord, listen to me.

---

[1] ben means "son of", see note on page 22.

I have given the field to you.
The cave in it I have also given to you.
In the presence of my compatriots
I give it to you, go and
Bury your dead."

Abraham bowed down low
Before the elders of the people of the land.
He spoke to Ephron in the hearing
Of the elders of the people of the land,
"If you would give it, hear me out,
I am going to give you money for the field.
Take it from me, and allow me to bury my dead there."

Ephron replied to Abraham with these words:
"My lord, now hear me out.
A piece of land worth four hundred silver shekels,[1]
Between me and you, of what significance is it?
Just bury your dead."

Abraham understood what Ephron was saying.
Abraham weighed out for Ephron the silver
Which he had mentioned in the hearing of the Hittites –
Four hundred shekels of silver acceptable to merchants.
Thus Ephron's field which was in Machpelah facing Mamre,
The field and the cave in it and all the trees in the field,
That were within its boundaries,
Were made sure as Abraham's possession
In the presence of the Hittites, the elders
And all who sat by the city gates.

After this transaction Abraham buried Sarah his wife
In the cave of the field of Machpelah
Facing Mamre – the same is Hebron – in the land of Canaan.
So it was that the field and the cave in it were sold

---

[1] A substantial sum considering that it would take a well-paid labourer fifty years to earn this amount.

By the Hittites to Abraham for a permanent possession
As a family place for burial.

Abraham was old, very advanced in years.
The LORD had blessed him in every way.
Abraham thought, "My death is approaching,
I must find a wife for Isaac, my son.
Perhaps I will live to see my grandchildren
Who will fulfil God's promise to me
That I will be a father to nations and
My descendants will be as many as the stars
That light up the heavens."

Abraham instructed the most senior servant of his household,
He who governed his entire estate,
"Place your hand under my thigh
[for this was the manner of making an oath].
I will make you swear, by the LORD the
God of the heavens and the God of the earth,
That you will not take a wife for my son
From the Canaanite women
In whose midst I dwell.
You shall proceed to my native land
To the land of my kinsmen.
From there you shall fetch
A wife for my son, Isaac.

The servant replied to him,
"What if the woman does not wish to follow me
To this land; shall I bring back your son
To the land from which you came?"
Abraham said to him, "Guard your thoughts
From taking my son back there.
The LORD, the God of the heavens
Who took me out of my father's house,
From the land of my kinsman,
Who spoke to me and promised me with these words,

'To your descendants will I give this land,'
He will send his Messenger before you;
You shall get a wife for my son from there.
If the woman will not wish to follow you,
You are released from this oath to me.
Just do not take my son back there."

Drink, I will also water your camels

The servant put his hand under the thigh
Of Abraham his master, and swore to him
That he would do as he was instructed.
The servant took ten camels from among his master's camels
And set off with the best of his master's possessions.
He departed for Aram Naharaim towards the city of Nahor,
After many days, he reached Aram Naharaim.
He made the camels kneel down by a well outside the city.
It was evening, the time when women went out to draw water.
He prayed, "O LORD, God of my master Abraham,
Give me, I pray, good fortune this day
And show kindness to my master, Abraham.
See, I am standing by the fountain.
The daughters of the city are coming to draw water.
Let it be that the girl to whom I will say:
'Please, lower your pitcher so that I may drink from it,'
Will respond, 'Drink, I will also water your camels.'
She is the one you have chosen for your servant, Isaac.
By this will I know that you have been kind to my master."
Even before he finished speaking Rebecca approached,
[Who was born to Bethuel, the son of Milcah,
the wife of Nahor,
Abraham's brother[1]] with her pitcher on her shoulder.
And the girl was very lovely to look at,
A virgin never touched by a man.

---

[1] Rebecca is Isaac's first cousin once removed.

She went down to the fountain,
Filled her pitcher and came up.
The servant ran to meet her. He said to her,
"Please give me a little water to drink from your pitcher."
She replied, "Drink, my lord." She quickly lowered the pitcher
To her hand so that she could let him drink.
When she had given him enough to drink, she said,
"I will also draw water for your camels
Until they too have had enough to drink."
She quickly emptied the water from her pitcher into the trough
And ran again to the well to draw water.
She drew water for all his camels.
The man looked at her piercingly, stunned in silence,
Wondering: had the LORD given him success or not?
When she finished watering the camels,
The man produced a golden ring weighing half a shekel
And two golden bracelets for her hands
Weighing ten shekels. He asked her,
"Whose daughter are you? Tell me, please, is there room in
Your father's house for us to lodge?" She replied,
"I am the daughter of Bethuel, Milcah's and Nahor's son."
She went on to say, "We have more than enough
Straw and provender and also room to sleep."
The man knew that the Lord had answered his prayer.
The man bowed his head and worshipped the LORD,
"Blessed be the LORD, the God of my master's kinsmen."
The girl ran to her mother's rooms
To tell them what happened.
Now Rebecca had a brother whose name was Laban.
Laban, **wasting no time**,
Ran to the man outside by the fountain,
Because he had seen the ring and the bracelets
On the hands of his sister and had heard the words
Of Rebecca, his sister: "Thus spoke the man to me."
He came to the man, standing with the camels by the well.
He said, "Come, O blessed of the LORD,

Why would you remain outside
As I have made the house ready for you
And room for the camels?"
He provided straw and provender for the camels and
Water to wash his feet and the feet of the
Men who were with him.

They put food before him, but he said,
"I will not eat until I say my piece." "Speak then," they said.
He began, "I am Abraham's manservant,
The LORD has blessed my master exceedingly.
He has become great. He has given him flocks and herds,
Silver, gold, male and female servants, camels and donkeys.
Sarah, my master's wife, bore a son to my master
After she was old. He has given him all he owns.
Now, my master made me take an oath to this effect:
'You will not take a wife for my son
From the Canaanite women
In whose land I dwell. But you will go to my father's house
To my family to take a wife for my son.'
I said to my master: 'Perhaps, the woman will not follow me.'
He reassured me, 'The LORD before whom I walk
Will send his Messenger with you. He will prosper your path
You will bring back a wife for my son
From my family, from my father's house.
Then you will be released of your oath
Once you contact my family.
If they will not give her to you
You are freed from your oath to me.'

Today I arrived at the fountain and I said
[For the man wanted to show Rebecca's family
That the hand of God supported his mission],
'O LORD, God of my master, Abraham,
If you would now prosper the road I am taking:
See I am standing by a fountain and
The woman who goes out to draw water to whom I say,

'Give me, please, a little water from your pitcher.'
And she will say to me, 'You shall drink,
But also for your camels will I draw water.'
She is the woman whom the LORD has
Chosen for my master's son.
Before I had finished thinking these thoughts, see
Rebecca approaches with a pitcher on her shoulder.
She goes down to the fountain to draw water.
I said to her, 'Please, give me water to drink.'
With alacrity she lowered her pitcher from her shoulder.
She said, 'Drink and I will also water your camels.'
I drank and she also watered the camels.

I enquired of her, 'Whose daughter are you?'
She answered, 'The daughter of Bethuel ben Nahor
Whom Milcah his wife had borne for him.'
I put a ring on her nose and bracelets on her wrists.
I bowed low to the LORD and
I blessed the LORD , the God of my master Abraham
Who led me faithfully on the path to take
The daughter[1] of my master's brother for his son.
Now, if you will act with true kindness towards my master,
Tell me, and if not, also tell me, so that
I will know whether to turn to the right or to the left.''

Laban (her brother) and Bethuel (her father) answered:
"From what you say, we see that this is God's will.
We are not able to express a view to you –
Favourable or unfavourable. Here is Rebecca!
Take her and go and let her become your master's son's wife
As the LORD has spoken.''

---

[1] As is the case with Abraham's claims that Sarah was his father's daughter,
here too 'daughter' is employed to mean granddaughter.

Isaac brought her into his mother Sarah's tent

When the manservant of Abraham heard their words,
He prostrated himself before the LORD.
The manservant brought out jewels of silver and
Jewels of gold and clothing to give Rebecca.
Precious gifts did he give her brother and mother[1].
They ate and drank, he and the men who were with him.
They went to sleep and got up in the morning.
He, the servant, said, "Send me off to my master!"
But her brother and mother said,
"Let the girl stay with us a year,
At least ten months; after that she will go."
He said to them, "Delay me not.
The LORD has prospered my way.
Send me off, so that I may go to my master."
They replied, "We will call the girl, and ask her to decide."
They summoned Rebecca and asked her,
"Will you go with this man?" She replied: "I will go."
So they sent away their sister and her nurse,
Along with Abraham's servant and his men.

They blessed Rebecca, saying to her:
"You are our sister,
Be the mother of a million.
May your descendants possess the cities of those who hate them."
Rebecca arose with her handmaidens.
They rode upon the camels and followed the manservant.
So did the manservant take Rebecca and go.

---

[1] The reader may be surprised that Rebecca's father is not a recipient of
Abraham's largesse; also that Laban takes precedence over Bethuel, his father,
when they address Abraham's emissary. This has led to the supposition that it
was a matriarchal structure where the son becomes his mother's spokesman.
This speculation is supported by Abraham's fear that the family would expect
the man to join the wife's family.

Isaac was coming from the direction of Beer-lahai-roi
[**The place to which Hagar had fled from Sarah's persecution**],
For he was living then in the land of the Negev.
Isaac was going for a walk in the fields towards evening.
He looked up and behold, he saw camels approaching.
Rebecca also looked up at that very moment.
She saw Isaac and alighted from the camel.
She said to the manservant,
"Who is this man who is walking across the field to greet us?"
The manservant answered: "He is my master."
She then took her veil and covered herself.

The manservant told Isaac all the things he had done.
Isaac brought her into his mother Sarah's tent.
He took Rebecca to be his wife.
He loved her.
Thus was Isaac comforted after his mother's death.

Now that Abraham had made Isaac his heir,
He did not wish his other sons to hinder him.
For Abraham **after Isaac's birth** took another woman.
Her name was Keturah. She bore him Zimran, Yokshan,
Medan, Midian, Ishbak and Shuah.
These are the children of Keturah.
Are their sons not recorded in the Book of Genealogies?[1]
Abraham had given all that he had to Isaac
But to the sons of the concubines which Abraham had
Abraham gave gifts; and he sent them away
From Isaac, his son,
While he was still alive, eastward to the land of Kedem.
Abraham would live to see the birth of Isaac's children,
Indeed to see Jacob and Esau become young men, but
These are the days and the years of Abraham's life.
He lived to be one hundred and seventy-five years old.
Abraham surrendered his spirit and died

---

[1] See appendix 2, for Genesis 25:2–5.

In a good old age, a very old and fulfilled man.
He was gathered to his ancestors.

Isaac and Ishmael, his sons, buried him
In the cave of Machpelah, in the field of
Ephron ben Zoar the Hittite, which is facing Mamre.
This is the field that Abraham bought from the Hittites.
There was Abraham buried with Sarah his wife.
After the death of Abraham, God blessed Isaac his son.
Isaac was living in Beer-lahai-roi.

Now as to the generations of Ishmael,
Abraham's son, whom Hagar the Egyptian, Sarah's handmaid,
Gave birth for him, **these are recorded in the Genealogies?**[1]
He had twelve sons, princes of nations.
These are the years of the life of Ishmael, at
One hundred and thirty-seven years
He would surrender his spirit and die
And be gathered unto his ancestors.
Ishmael's descendants dwelt from Havila to Shur,
That is before Egypt as when you go towards Assyria.
They settled in the midst of all their kinsmen.

Two nations are in your belly

This is the history of Isaac, the son of Abraham.
It was after his name had been changed from Abram to
Abraham **[Father of many nations] that he** sired Isaac.
Isaac was forty years old when he took Rebecca,
The daughter of Bethuel the Aramean of Paddan-aram,[2]
The sister of Laban, the Aramean, to be his wife.

Isaac implored the LORD on behalf of his wife
For she was barren. The LORD responded to his plea.
Rebecca his wife conceived.

[1] See appendix 3, for Genesis 25:13–16.
[2] Identical with Aram Naharaim and Mesopotamia.

The children struggled together inside her
So that she said, "If this is the way it is going to be,
Why should I live?" She went to an oracle of the LORD.
The LORD told her:
"Two nations are in your belly
Two peoples shall be divided
Straight out of your womb.
One people shall be stronger than the other.
The elder shall serve the younger."

The days of her pregnancy came to an end
As **the Lord had said,** there were twins in her belly.
The first came out ruddy, all hairy like a garment.
And they named him Esau [hairy].
Afterwards, out comes his brother,
His hand grasping the heel [ekev] of Esau.
They named him Jacob [grasping the heel].
Isaac was sixty years old when she gave birth to them.

The boys grew up. Esau was a good hunter, an outdoors man.
Jacob was quiet, an indoors man.
Isaac loved Esau because of the venison he brought him.
But Rebecca loved Jacob.
Jacob once made some soup.
Esau came in from the hunt, exhausted.
Esau told Jacob, "Feed me, please
With this very red soup, for I am very tired."
Therefore he was also called: Edom [red].
But Jacob said, "In exchange for your birthright!"
Esau replied, **"Because of the perils of the hunt,**
I am always in danger of death.
What good to me is the birthright?"
But Jacob insisted, "Swear me an oath now."
He swore an oath to him and sold his birthright to Jacob.
So Jacob gave Esau bread and lentil soup.
He ate and drank, stood up and went away.
In this way did Esau discount his birthright.

There was another famine in the land in addition to
The first famine which occurred in the time of Abraham.
Isaac went to Abimelech,[1]
King of the Philistines at Gerar.
Isaac had thought to go to Egypt as had Abraham.
The LORD appeared to him and said,
"Do not go down to Egypt.
Settle in the place which I tell you.
Dwell in this land
For I will be with you and bless you.
Because I will give you and your descendants
All these lands and I will fulfil the oath
Which I swore to Abraham, your father.
I will make your descendants as
Numerous as the stars of the heavens.
I will give to your descendants all these lands.
As your descendants are blessed, so will all the
Nations of the earth ask to be blessed.
This is because Abraham heard my voice.
He obeyed my charges, my commandments,
My rites and my instructions."
So Isaac stayed in Gerar.

The men of the place, **fancying her,** asked about his wife.
He replied, "She is my sister,"
Because he was afraid to say: 'My wife'
Lest the men of the place kill him,
Because of Rebecca, for she was lovely to look at.
After he had been there a long time,
Abimelech, king of the Philistines,
Looked out of the window.

[1] Possibly the kings of Gerar were always called Abimelech [Hebrew meaning: my father is Moloch – a Canaanite god] as the kings of Egypt were called Pharaohs. Otherwise it would be strange that the same king could have been deceived by both Abraham and his son Isaac after an interim of some sixty years.

He saw Isaac teasing Rebecca, his wife.
So, Abimelech summoned Isaac and chastised him,
"Is she not your wife but did you not say she was your sister?"
Isaac explained to him, "I said this because
I feared for my life because of her **beauty.**"
Abimelech replied, "What is this you have done?
One of the men might have slept with your wife
And brought guilt upon us."
Abimelech commanded the men, saying,
"Anyone who touches this man or his wife will die!"

Isaac farmed in that land, and
He found that in that year he had profited a hundred fold.
For the LORD had blessed him. The man grew rich,
He became richer and powerful; he became exceedingly great.
He had many flocks and many herds and a great household.
The Philistines envied him.
All the wells which his father's servants had dug
In the days of Abraham, his father,
The Philistines had sealed up by filling them with earth.
Abimelech, **seeing the enmity against Isaac,**
Said to Isaac, "You had better leave us,
Because you are too powerful for us."
So Isaac left that place.
He set up camp and dwelt there in the river bed of Gerar.
Isaac re-dug the wells which had been dug
In the days of Abraham, his father,
Which the Philistines had closed up after Abraham's death.
He gave them the same names as had his father.
Isaac's servants dug in the river bed
And found there a well of sweet water.
The herdsmen of Gerar fought with those of Isaac,
Claiming, "The water is ours!"
So he named the well: "Contention",
Because they contended with him.
They dug another well over which they also fought.

So he called its name: "Enmity".
He moved camp from there and dug another well.
Because they did not fight over it,
He named it "Wide and broad".
For he thought, "Now that the LORD has enlarged my space,
We shall be prosperous in the land."
And he moved on from there to Beersheba.

The LORD appeared to him that night saying,
"I am the God of Abraham, your father.
Do not fear, for I am with you.
I will bless you and increase your descendants
For the sake of Abraham, my servant."
He built an altar there
And invoked the name of the LORD.
He set up camp there; Isaac's servants dug a well there.
Now Abimelech came from Gerar to see him.
With Ahuzzath,[1] one of his friends, and Phicol,
The chief of his troops. Isaac reproached them,
"Why have you come to me since you hate me,
And sent me away from you?" They answered:
"We certainly know that the LORD was with you.
We thought, 'Let there be an oath between us,
Between us and between you.'
We will make a pact with you,
That you will do us no harm
Just as we did not harm you, but treated you well,
Sending you away in peace.
You know you are blessed by the LORD."
So they made a feast for themselves.
They ate and drank. They woke up in the morning,

---

[1] As Phicol means "Voice of All", symbolic of his being representative of all the Philistines, the name of the friend Ahuzzath means possession and symbolically reflects that the Philistines are seeking to claim sovereignty over Beersheba though it is not part of Philistia. Abraham recognized their rule over it but Isaac did not.

Swore peace to each other and
Isaac saw them off in friendship.
On that very day, Isaac's servants arrived and told him
About a well they had dug, saying to him:
"We found water." He named the place : "Oath".
For this reason the city is called "Oath-well" to this day.[1]

Esau was forty years old when he took to wife
Judith, daughter of Beeri, the Hittite;
And Basemath, the daughter of Elan, the Hittite.
They were a dark cloud over the lives of Isaac and Rebecca.

The voice is the voice of Jacob

When Isaac became old and his eyesight was blurred,
He summoned Esau, his elder son,
"My son, behold I am now an old man.
I do not know the day of my death.
So now get your gear together, your bow and arrows.
Go out into the wilds and bring me venison,
Make a tasty dish for me such as I love.
Bring it to me so that I may eat.
In return, my soul will bless you before I die.

Rebecca listened to what Isaac said to Esau, his son.
Esau went out to the fields to hunt for venison.
Rebecca said to Jacob, her son,
"Listen, I heard your father speaking
To Esau, your brother. He said, 'Bring me venison,
Make me a tasty dish and I will eat it,
And bless you before the LORD before I die.'
Now, my son, listen to what I say.

---

[1] Hebrew is Beersheba. Abraham had previously also sworn an oath of peace
with Abimelech at the same place, and on that account, it is also called at that
time Beersheba. Was the author working with two traditions as to which
Patriarch named the place?

Do what I tell you. Go now to the flocks,
Fetch from there two good kids from the goats.
I will make of them a tasty dish
For your father, just as he likes.
You will take it to your father. He will eat.
In return he will bless you before his death."

Jacob said to Rebecca, his mother,
"Surely my brother is a hairy man
And I am smooth-skinned.
Perhaps, my father will feel me
And see that I am a deceiver.
Will I not bring upon myself a curse
Rather than a blessing?"
His mother answered him, "Upon me be your curse, my son.
Just listen to what I say. Go and fetch them for me!"
He went; he fetched; he brought them to his mother.
His mother made tasty dishes which his father liked.
Rebecca fetched good clothing belonging to Esau,
Her elder son, which was with her in the house.
She dressed Jacob, her younger son.
The skins of the kids of the goats she put on his hands,
Upon the smooth sides of his neck.
She put the tasty meat and the bread she had baked
Into the hands of Jacob, her son.

When he came to his father, he said, "My father."
"Yes, who are you, my son?" he asked.
Jacob replied to his father, "I am Esau, your first born,
I have fulfilled your request. Now, sit up, please.
Eat my venison that your soul may bless me."
Isaac said to his son, "How is this, my son?
You were quick to find **the deer, to kill and prepare it.**"
"Because the LORD your God," he replied,
"Sent me good speed." But Isaac said to Jacob,
"Come close, please, that I may feel you, my son:
Are you really Esau my son or not?"

Jacob approached Isaac his father and he felt him
And he thought, "The voice, it is the voice of Jacob
But the hands, they are the hands of Esau."
He did not recognize him because his hands were as hairy
As his brother Esau's hands. So he was prepared to bless him.
He asked, "Are you really my son Esau?"
He answered: "I am."
He said, "Bring the meal to me, I will eat my son's venison
So that my soul may bless you."
He brought it near to him and he ate.
He brought him wine and he drank.
Isaac, his father, said to him,
"Come close and kiss me, my son."
He came close and kissed him.
Isaac smelt the smell of his clothes and blessed him,
Saying, "See, the smell of my son
Is the smell of the field
Which the LORD has blessed.
Let God give you the dew of heaven
And the fatness of the earth
And plenty of corn and wine.
Let peoples serve you and
Nations bow down to you.
Be a lord over your kindred **nations.**
Let the sons of your mother bow down to you.
Cursed be those who seek to do you harm
And blessed be those who do you good."

Just as Isaac finished blessing Jacob –
Barely had Jacob withdrawn from Isaac his father's presence –
Then Esau, his brother, came with his venison.
He too had prepared a tasty meal to bring to his father.
He said to his father, "Let my father get up,
Let him eat from his son's venison
So that his soul may bless me."
Isaac, his father, asked him, "Who are you?"

He replied, "I am your son, your first born, Esau!"
Isaac started to shiver and tremble violently.
He could not stop. But he shouted out,
"From where did this venison come,
Who brought it to me, that which I ate
Before you came; and I blessed him?
Yes, and now he will be blessed."

Have you no spare blessing for me?

When Esau heard his father's words
He let out a great and bitter howl
Which did not end, crying out to his father,
"Bless me, even me, my father." He replied,
"Your brother came in stealth and took your blessing."
He said, "No wonder he was named Jacob.
Twice he has supplanted me.[1]
He took away my birthright
And now, he has stolen my blessing."
He cried: "Have you no spare blessing for me?"

Isaac answered Esau: "I have made him lord over you.
I have given to him all his kinsmen as servants,
I have blessed him with sustenance of corn and wine.
What can I now do for you, my son?"
Esau asked his father, "Father, do you only have one blessing?
Bless me too!" Again he sobbed loudly and wept.
Isaac, his father, answered him,
"You shall not live in the fat places of the earth
Nor in places blessed with dew from heaven.
By your sword, you will live.
You will serve your brother,
But the time will come when you will break loose
And remove his yoke from your neck."

---

[1] Literally, to grab by the heel to overtake.

When Isaac heard what Rebecca, his wife, had done,
He said to her, "What have you done to me,
To steal my blessing from Esau for Jacob?
You have cheated me and Esau, and
Jacob, our son, has become a deceiver of God and man."
Rebecca answered, "Esau sold his birthright to Jacob.
Your blessing by right belonged to Jacob.
Did not the Lord also tell me when I enquired of him,
Two nations will divide themselves out of your womb,
And the older will serve the younger?
It was God's will that Jacob be blessed by you.
See, our son Esau has married Canaanite women.
Now, Jacob will marry a woman from our kinsmen
And be a comfort to us in our old age."

But Esau hated Jacob because of the blessing
His father had given him. He said to himself:
"Once the days of mourning for my father are over
I will kill Jacob, my brother."
The thoughts of Esau her elder son were told to Rebecca.
She sent and called Jacob, her younger son,
"Look, Esau your brother does comfort himself
With the thought of killing you.
Now, listen to what I tell you:
Go, escape to Laban, my brother in Haran.
You can stay with him for several years,
Until your brother's anger subsides.
When your brother is no longer angry with you
And he forgets what you did to him,
I will send and bring you back from there.
Why should I mourn for you both in one day?"

**Rebecca did not tell Isaac of Esau's words,
Or her instructions to Jacob to flee for his safety.**
Rebecca said to Isaac, "I am weary to death
Because of the daughters of the Hittites.
If Jacob takes to wife a Hittite woman,

Such as these Hittite women that Esau has married,
What use is my life?"

Isaac summoned Jacob **and was reconciled to him**.
He blessed him and instructed him with these words:
"You must not take a wife from the daughters of Canaan.
Arise and get you to Paddan-aram,
To the house of Bethuel, your mother's father,
And there take a wife from the daughters of Laban,
Your mother's brother. God Shaddai will bless you.
He will make you fruitful and increase **your issue**.
You will become a community of nations.
He will give you the blessing of Abraham,
To you, and to your descendants after you
To give you as your inheritance the land in which you reside,
The land which God promised to give to Abraham."

Then Isaac sent Jacob off to go to Paddan-Aram,
To Laban, the son of Bethuel the Aramean,
The brother of Rebecca, Jacob and Esau's mother.
Esau saw that Isaac had blessed Jacob again,
Sending him to Paddan-aram to take a wife from there,
That when he blessed him, he ordered him thus:
"Do not take a wife from the daughters of Canaan."
Jacob obeyed his father and his mother
And went off to Paddan-aram.
Esau realized that Isaac his father
Did not like the women of Canaan.
So Esau went to Ishmael, and took to wife
In addition to his other wives
Mahalath, the daughter of Ishmael, the son of Abraham,
She was the sister of Nebaioth,
So did Esau seek to win his father's approval.

The Lord is in this place

Jacob left Beersheba to go to Haran.
He came to the place[1]
And stopped there because the sun had set.
He took one of the stones of the place to lay under his head.
He slept in the place. He dreamt and look –
A ladder is standing on the ground
With its top touching the heavens.
And see – Messengers of God
Are going up and down on it.
And behold – the LORD is standing above him.
He spoke: "I am the LORD,
The God of Abraham, your father,[2]
And the God of Isaac.
The ground on which you sleep
I will give to you and your descendants.
Your descendants will be as the dust of the earth.
Your issue will spread out westward to the sea,
Eastwards, northwards and southwards to the Negev.
All the families of the earth will ask
To be blessed as are your descendants.
Know that I am with you
To watch over you wherever you go,
To bring you back to this land,
For I will not forsake you until
I perform what I promise you."

Jacob was startled out of his sleep.
He said, "Surely the LORD is in this place
And I was ignorant of it."
He was terrified and thought,
"How full of awe is this place!

---

[1] It is called "the place" not "a place" in recognition of its holiness which is soon to be revealed.

[2] Abraham, not Isaac, is his key ancestor, so he is referred to as his father.

This must be God's house.
This must be the gateway of heaven."
When Jacob woke up in the morning,
He took the stone which was lying under his head,
Set it up as a pillar and poured oil on the top of it.
He called the name of that place Bethel [The House of God].
The former name of the city was Luz.

Jacob made a vow, saying,
"If God will be with me and watch over me,
On this path which I take
And gives me food to eat and clothes to wear,
So that I return safely to my father's house,
Then the LORD will be my God and
This stone which I have erected as a pillar
Will be God's House. All that you give me,
I will give a tenth to you."

Jacob picked himself up and went
To the land of the people of the east.
Suddenly he saw a well in the field.
He saw three flocks of sheep lying by it
For it was from that well that the flocks were watered.
There was a large boulder on the mouth of the well.
When all the flocks were gathered there,
The shepherds would roll off the stone from the well
And water the flocks. They then returned the boulder
To its place on top of the well.

They passed for him like a few days

Jacob spoke to them, "My brothers, where do you come from?"
They answered, "We are from Haran." He asked them,
"Do you know Laban, ben[1] Nahor?" They replied, "We do."

---

[1] Laban was Nahor's grandson, but Nahor was the head of the household.
Jacob refers to him as he would be better known than Bethuel, Laban's father.

He asked them, "Is he well?" They answered, "He is fine,
In fact, here comes his daughter, Rachel, with the sheep."
He asked, "**I do not understand.** It is only high noon,
Not time for collecting the flocks together.
Why don't you water the sheep and lead them to pasture?"
They replied, "We cannot until all the herds gather.
Then they, **all the herdsmen,** roll away the boulder
From the well's mouth. Then they water the sheep."
While he was speaking to them, Rachel came with her
Father's sheep because she was a shepherdess.
When Jacob saw Rachel, the daughter of Laban,
His mother's brother
And the sheep of Laban, his uncle, Jacob went and
Singlehandedly rolled the boulder off the top of
The well and watered the flocks of Laban,
Jacob **took her in his arms and** kissed Rachel.
He cried **with happiness** and wept **tears of joy.**
Jacob then explained to Rachel that
He was her father's kinsman,
Because he was Rebecca's son. She ran to tell her father, and
When Laban heard the news of Jacob, his nephew, he ran to
Greet him. He hugged and kissed him
And brought him to his house.
He described to Laban all that had happened to him.
Laban declared to him, "Are you not my bone and flesh?
You will stay with me." He lived with him for a month.
Rising early and tending the flocks with the sons of Laban.

Laban said to Jacob, "Because you are my kin,
Should you work for me for nothing?
Tell me what wages you want."
Laban had two daughters,
The name of the older one was Leah,
The name of the younger was Rachel.
The eyes of Leah were without sparkle,

Rachel was lovely to look at.
Indeed a beauty to behold.
Jacob loved Rachel, so he said,
"I will work for you seven years
For Rachel, your younger daughter."
Laban replied, "It is better that I give her to you
Than to another man. Stay with me. **It will be as you say.**"

Jacob worked for Laban for seven years.
They passed for him like a few days
Because of his great love for her.
Jacob said to Laban, "Give me my wife,
For my days of labour have been fulfilled.
Let me go to her."

Laban thought to himself,
"Where shall I find a husband for Leah?
And where shall I find such a good worker?
On his wedding night I will ply him with wine
And give him Leah in Rachel's place."
He told Leah what he was about to do.
She protested, "But, father, he will hate me.
My sister too will hate me for she loves Jacob."
Laban answered her: "He will forgive you
For it is my doing. Jacob will have Rachel too."
Rachel was guarded in her mother's house.
Leah was dressed and perfumed
And a veil covered her face.
Laban invited all the men of the place to a feast.
It happened at night, **when Jacob was filled with wine,**
He took Leah, his daughter, and brought her to him.
He made love to her.
[Laban gave Zilpah, his maidservant, to Leah
His daughter, to be her maid.]
When morning came, see, it was Leah!
He **rushed out and** demanded of Laban:
"What is this that you have done to me?

It was for Rachel that I worked for you!
Why have you cheated me?"
Laban answered, "It is not done here
To give **to wife** the younger before the firstborn.
Complete this week of wedding festivities,
Then I will give you the other one too,
For the labour that you will do for me
For yet another seven years."

Jacob agreed to do this.
The week **of festivities** for her were completed.
Then Laban gave him Rachel to be his wife.
[Laban gave Rachel Bilhah, his servant, to be her maid.]
Jacob slept with Rachel and he loved her more than Leah.
So he worked a further seven years.

Jacob thought to himself,
"What my mother and I did to my father, Isaac,
In stealing from him Esau's blessing,
Leah and Laban, her father, have done to me.
They stole Rachel on my wedding night.
God has punished me for my deception."
Whenever he looked upon Leah, he was angry with her
Because she deceived him, and cheated her sister
And made him remember what he did to Esau, his brother.

The LORD saw that Leah was hated
So he opened her womb; but Rachel was barren.
Leah conceived **on the night of her wedding**
And gave birth to a son.
She named him Reuben [see: a son]
Because she thought, "The LORD has seen
My affliction. Now my husband will love me
For giving him a son." **When Jacob saw that**
Rachel was barren, he slept with Leah.
She conceived again and gave birth to a son.
She said, "Because the LORD heard that I am hated,

He has also given me this child.
She, therefore, named him Simeon [hearing].

She conceived again and gave birth to a son,
And said, "Surely this time my husband
Will become bonded to me because
I have borne him three sons."
Therefore, she named him Levi [bonding].
She conceived yet again and gave birth to a son.
"This time I will praise the LORD."
Therefore, she named him Judah [praise].
After Judah, she stopped bearing sons.

Am I in the place of God?

When Rachel saw that she could not bear children for Jacob,
Rachel envied her sister. She cried out to Jacob,
"Give me children. If not, let me die!"
Jacob became angry with Rachel. He said,
"Am I in the place of God, the One
Who has withheld from you the fruit of the womb?"
Rachel **thought again and** said, **as did Sarah to
Jacob's grandfather, Abraham,** "Here is my handmaid,
Bilhah. Sleep with her. She will give birth on my knees.
I too, through her, will build a household."
She gave him Bilhah, her maid, to be his concubine.
Jacob slept with her. Bilhah conceived and bore him a son.
Rachel said, "God has judged me, and has also heard my cry.
He has given me a son." So she named him Dan [judge].
She conceived again and Bilhah, Rachel's handmaid,
Gave birth to a second son for Jacob. Rachel declared,
"A contest of the gods have I waged with my sister.
I have been victorious." She named him Naphtali [my contest].

Leah realized that she had stopped bearing children.
She took Zilpah, her maid, and gave her to Jacob to be
His concubine. Zilpah, the maid of Leah, bore Jacob a son.

Leah exclaimed, "Good fortune has come."
She named him Gad [fortune]. Zilpah bore Jacob a second son.
Leah said, "How happy am I, for the women will say
I am happy." So she named him Asher [happiness].

Reuben was walking about during the wheat harvest,
He found mandrakes in the field
And took them to Leah, his mother.
Rachel begged Leah, "Please give me your son's mandrakes."[1]
She refused, "Is it not enough that you have taken my
Husband? Would you also take my son's mandrakes?"
Rachel said, "What if he will sleep with you tonight
In exchange for your son's mandrakes?"
When Jacob returned from the fields in the evening,
Leah ran out to greet him, saying, "You will sleep with me
Because I have hired you with my son's mandrakes."
He slept with her on that night, and God heard Leah's wish.
She conceived and bore Jacob a fifth son.
Leah said, "God has given me my reward
In that I gave my handmaid to my husband."
So she gave him the name Issacher [reward].
Leah conceived again and bore Jacob a sixth son.
Leah said, "God has given me a good dowry.
Now my husband will honour me for I have given him six sons."
And she named him Zebulun [honour].
Afterwards she bore a daughter.
She called her by the name of Dinah.

God remembered Rachel's plight
And heard her prayers.
He opened her womb; she conceived and bore a son.
She said, "God has taken away my disgrace."[2]

[1] Considered to be a fertility potion.
[2] Barrenness was one of God's severest punishments for to be without a child was to be deprived of immortality.

She named him Joseph [add] because she hoped,
"Let the LORD give me another son."

At the time when Rachel bore Joseph,
Jacob had completed another seven years of labour.
Jacob said to Laban, "Allow me to leave.
Let me return to my place and to my land.
Grant me my wives and my children
For whom I served you and let me go,
For you know the value of my work –
How I served you." Laban replied to him.
"If you can find it in your heart, stay,
For I have seen the signs.
The LORD has blessed me because of you.
Decide your own wages and I will pay it."
He replied, "You know how well I have served you,
And how well your cattle grew under my care.
Because you had little before I came
But its increase has been manifold.
As you have said, the LORD has blessed you because of me.
Now, when will I look after my own house?"
He asked, "What shall I give you? **Name your price.**"
Jacob answered, "You will not give me anything.
Only agree to do this thing and I will remain
To pasture your flock and to watch over it.
I will today survey your entire flock,
Removing from it every speckled and spotted lamb
And every black lamb among the sheep.
The spotted and speckled among the goats.
They shall be my wages.
So will my honesty be evident hereafter
In regard to my wages that you have agreed.
Any lamb or goat which is not speckled and spotted
Among the goats or black among the sheep
Shall be counted as stolen by me,
If I have put them among my own herds."

Genesis 30:34–43

Laban considered how few were the speckled and spotted,
Because most of the sheep were white and goats black.
Laban said, "That is fair, let it be as you say."
During that day **to give himself a further advantage,**
He removed all the spotted and speckled she-goats,
Every one that had white on it, and all the black sheep –
These he entrusted to his sons. He put three days' journey
Between himself and Jacob.
Jacob pastured the rest of Laban's flocks,
The sheep that were white and the black goats.

Jacob took fresh roots of poplar, almond and plane trees.
He peeled white streaks in them
To expose the whiteness of the shoots.
He stuck the shoots which he had peeled in the troughs
At the watering places where the flocks came to drink,
Facing the flocks when in heat they came to drink.[1]
The flocks thus mated in front of the shoots and **in time**
The flocks bred ring-streaked, speckled and spotted lambs.
Then Jacob separated the lambs **and during their mating**
Set the faces of the flock towards the ring-streaked
And all the black in the flock of Laban.
He then set his own speckled herds apart,
And kept them separate from Laban's flock.
Also, whenever the stronger of the flock were mating,
Jacob placed the shoots in the troughs
In the sight of the flocks, so that
They conceived among the speckled shoots.
With the weaker sheep, he did not do this:
So the weaker sheep and goats, white and black,
Were Laban's and the stronger were Jacob's.
So the man's wealth increased greatly, and
He had not only large flocks, but also

[1] A superstition which prevails even today, that the appearance of embryos can be influenced by what their mothers see during conception.

Maids and menservants and camels and asses,
Which he purchased through the increase of his herds.

Your father cheated me

The words of Laban's sons came to his attention:
"Jacob has taken all that which belonged to our father,
From our father he has achieved all this wealth!"
Jacob also noted that his demeanor towards him
Was not as it had been in the past.
The Lord then said to Jacob, "Return to your father's land,
To your birthplace, and I will be with you."[1]
Jacob sent a messenger to call Rachel and Leah
To the field where he was attending his herds.
He explained to them, "I look at your father's face.
It is not as it used to be. **He wishes me no good.**
But fortunately, the God of my father has been with me.
You know that with what complete dedication
I worked for your father, but your father cheated me.
He changed my wages ten times.
But God did not let him harm me.
If he spoke thus, 'The speckled will be your wages,'
All the flocks bore speckled young, but if he spoke thus,
'The striped will be your wages,' all the flocks bore striped.
In this way God has taken away your father's cattle
And given them to me. At the time when the flocks
Were mating, I looked up and saw a vision:
Look and see, the he-goats which leaped
Upon the females were striped, speckled and mottled.
And a Messenger from God said to me in the vision,
'Jacob.' I replied, 'Here I am.' He said,
'Look and see: all the he-goats leaping on the she-goats

[1] The divine command to leave immediately following Jacob's apprehension
may suggest that in ancient days any deep conviction about a course of action
may have been interpreted or even heard as the voice of God.

Are striped, speckled and mottled. **I made this happen,**
Because I have seen all that Laban is doing to you.
I am the God of Bethel
Where you anointed a pillar,
Where you swore an oath to me.
Now, get you gone from this land
Return to the land of your birth'"[1]

Rachel and Leah answered him as one:
"Do we have any portion or inheritance
In our father's house?
Does he not consider us as strangers?
For he has sold us and eaten up our dowry.
All the wealth which God has taken from our father,
It is ours and our children's!
No, do whatever God has told you."
Jacob proceeded to place his children and wives on camels.
He led away all his cattle, everything he possessed –
The cattle he had acquired in Paddan-aram
To go to Isaac his father in the land of Canaan.

At this time, Laban had gone to shear his sheep.
Rachel **saw her opportunity and** stole the images
Of household gods which were her father's.
Jacob also slipped away from Laban the Aramean
Without telling him that he was running away.
He fled with everything he owned.
He proceeded to cross the river **Euphrates,**
Going in the direction of Mount Gilead.
Three days later Laban was informed that Jacob had fled.
He gathered his kinsmen and pursued him for seven days.
He overtook them at Mount Gilead.

God appeared to Laban the Aramean in a dream at night.
He said, "Take care. Do not speak to Jacob either good or evil.

---

[1] Jacob enlarges on the previous brief description of God's command to return home. Is Jacob seeking to impress his wives?

Do not threaten him, nor flatter him with sweet words,
Do not prevent him from returning to his father's house."

Laban caught up with Jacob who had encamped in the hills.
Laban with his kinsmen were also encamped on Mount Gilead.
Laban questioned Jacob, "What have you done?
To steal yourself away from me, to lead my daughters away
As though they were captives by the sword of war?
Why did you flee secretly, to steal away from me,
And not to tell me? Had I known
I would have sent you off joyously –
With songs, with the music of tambourines and harps –
You have not enabled me to kiss my sons
And daughters **goodbye.** Now, I ask you,
Have you not behaved irrationally?
It was in my power to do you harm,
But only last night, the God of your father said to me,
'You! Beware, speak neither good or evil to Jacob.'
Now that you feel compelled to be gone
Because you deeply long for your father's house,
Is this a reason for stealing my gods?"
Jacob replied to Laban with these words:
"As to the secrecy of my departure, I was afraid
That you would take away your daughters by force.
But, as to stealing your gods, I know nothing.
With whomever you find your gods, he shall not live; before
Our kinsmen see what is yours in my keeping and take it."
Because Jacob did not know that Rachel had stolen them.

Laban went through Jacob's and Leah's tents and
The tents of the two maidservants and found nothing.
When they left Leah's tent, they entered Rachel's.
Now Rachel had taken the images
And put them into her camel's saddle bag.
She was reclining on them.
Laban felt about the whole tent but found nothing.
She said to her father, "Let not my lord be angry

For I am not able to stand up before you,
For the way of women is upon me."
He continued to search but did not find the images.

Now Jacob was angry and he confronted Laban,
"What have I done wrong? What is my crime?" he demanded.
"That you have come after me in hot pursuit?
You have felt every piece of my furniture,
And what of your own items have you found?
Set them before my kinsmen and yours.
Let them judge between the two of us.
It is now twenty years that I have been with you.
Your ewes and she-goats have not miscarried.
The rams of your flocks have I not eaten.
That which was ravaged by beasts, I did not bring to you.
I took responsibility for the loss.
You held me accountable **for every lost head**
Whether it was stolen from me by day or night.
Thus was my life: the drought ate me up by day,
And the frost by night. Sleep fled from my eyes.
These twenty years in your house have I served you.
Fourteen years for your two daughters
And six years' **wages** for **shepherding** your flocks.
You have changed my wages ten times.
If the God of my father, the god of Abraham,
The Awesome God of Isaac was not with me,
You would have sent me away empty-handed.
God saw how I was exploited
And the sweat of my hands.
So he gave you warning last night."

Laban answered, saying to Jacob: **"In spite of what you say,**
The daughters are my daughters,
The children are my children,
The flocks are my flocks,
All that you see is mine.
As Patriarch, I possess all.

As for my daughters, what shall I do for them today
Or for their children which they have borne?
Come now, let us make a pact, I and you,
Let it be for a testimony between me and you."

Jacob took a boulder and set it up as a pillar.
Jacob said to his kinsmen, "Gather stones."
They did so and made it into a mound.
They ate there around the mound of stones.
Laban named it: Tegar-sahaduta, but Jacob called it Gal-ed.[1]
Laban said, "Today this mound is witness
Between me and you."
Therefore, its name is Gilead. Also Mizpah[2] for he said, "The
LORD watch between me and you
When we are far from each other.
If you oppress my daughters by taking
Wives over my daughters,
No man being witness for us,
See that God is the witness between me and you."
Laban continued, "See this mound and
This pillar which I have set up
Between me and you. The mound is a witness.
This pillar is a witness. I will not pass over this mound
To do you harm, nor will you pass over
This mound and this pillar to do me harm.
The God of Abraham and the God of Nahor
Will judge between us."
Jacob swore also by the Awesome God of Isaac, his father.
Jacob made a sacrifice on the mount.
He summoned his kinsmen to eat food together.
They ate a meal and slept on the mountain.
Laban woke up in the morning,
Kissed his grandsons and his daughters.
He blessed them and returned to his place.

---

[1] Both names mean 'the mound of stones is witness'.
[2] Meaning 'Watch over'.

Jacob too went on his way.
Messengers from God met him.
When Jacob saw them, he said,
"This is God's company." He named that place Mahanaim[1]
When Rachel confessed that she stole her father's gods
Jacob was very angry, "Why did you do such a thing?"
She said, "I did not want to leave my birthplace
Without my father's gods to protect me."
Jacob was silent because of his love for her.

And four hundred men are with him

Jacob sent messengers before him to Esau, his brother,
Into the Land of Seir, the fields of Edom.
He commanded them: "This is what you will say
To my lord Esau, 'Thus says your servant Jacob,
I have lived with Laban and stayed until now.
I have oxen and donkeys and flocks
And menservants and maidservants and I have
Sent messengers ahead to inform my lord
And to seek his favour.'"
The messengers returned to Jacob and told him,
"We came to your brother Esau.
He is also coming to greet you,
And four hundred men are with him."

Jacob was terrified and distraught.
He divided the people with him and
The flocks and the herds and the camels into two camps,
Thinking: "If Esau should come to attack one camp,
The remaining camp will escape."
Then Jacob prayed: "The God of my father Abraham,
The God of my father Isaac, the LORD who said to me,
'Go back to your country and your birthplace.

[1] Meaning 'two companies'.

I will look after you,'
I am not worthy of any of your kindnesses or
Of any of your acts of faithfulness
Which you have done for your servant.
Only with my staff I crossed the Jordan
And now I have become two encampments.
Deliver me, I pray, from the might of Esau,
From my brother's power, for I fear him,
Lest he come to smite mothers with their children.
Surely you said, 'I will make you prosperous
And as numerous as the sands of the sea,
Which are too great to count."'

He slept there that night
And took of what he possessed
A present for Esau, his brother.
200 she-goats and 20 he-goats, 200 ewes and 20 rams,
30 milch camels with their colts,
40 cows and 10 bulls, 20 she-asses and 10 he-asses.
He put these in the charge of his servants
Separating each drove from the other and
He told his servants, "Go ahead before me,
Keep a good distance between drove and drove."
He ordered the servants in the front line as follows:
"When my brother Esau meets you and asks you,
'Who are you, where are you going,
And to whom do these animals before you belong?'
This is what you are to say, 'They are Jacob's your servant,
It is a present sent to my lord Esau, and he,
My master, himself, is coming behind us."'
He instructed the second and third shepherds, indeed
All the shepherds that followed the droves;
"In this manner you shall speak to Esau
When you come across him, never omitting the words,
'And your servant Jacob himself is coming behind us."'
For he thought, "I will appease him with the presents

Which go in advance of me. Then when I face him,
Perhaps he will be kind to me **and forgive me.**"
So the presents went ahead before him,
He himself remained in the camp that night.

That night he proceeded to assemble his two wives,
His two handmaids and eleven sons, and
Crossed over the ford of the Jabbok.
After taking them across the stream,
He sent across all that belonged to him.
Jacob's **decision** was **to be** left on his own.
A Man wrestled with him until the break of dawn.
He saw that he could not defeat him.
He touched the hollow of his thigh and
The hollow of Jacob's thigh was wrenched
As he wrestled with him.
He said, "Let me go, for dawn is breaking."
He replied, "I will not let you go
Unless you bless me."
– "What is your name?"
– "Jacob."
– "No longer will Jacob be your name but Israel[1]
  Because you have fought with
  God and with men and you have been victorious."
– "Now, please tell me your name!"
– "Why do you seek to know my name?"
There he blessed him **and left him.**
Jacob named the place Peniel [face of God],
"Because I saw God face to face
And I am still alive!"

The sun shone for him as he passed through Peniel.
He limped because of an injury to his thigh.
Because of this, the Children of Israel do not eat

---

[1] Meaning uncertain, perhaps, 'He will fight with God', or 'God's champion'.

The vein of [a cow's] thigh even to this very day.[1]
Because he, the man of God, touched the
Hollow of Jacob's thigh in the hip socket.

I have seen the face of God

As his camp was moving on Jacob looked up and there –
Esau was fast approaching and with him the 400 men.
He divided the children of Leah, Rachel and the handmaids.
He placed the handmaids and their children in the front line
And Leah and her children behind them
And Rachel and Joseph at the very rear.
He thought, "If Esau has no mercy on mothers and children
But slays them, Rachel and Joseph might flee."
Jacob, however, went at the head of them all,
Seven times did he prostrate himself to the ground
Until he reached his brother.
Esau ran to greet him
And embraced him.
Laid his head upon his neck and kissed him.
Both of them wept.
When he raised his head, he saw the women and children.
He asked, "Who are these with you?"
He replied, "The children whom
God has given to your servant."
Then the handmaidens came near to Esau,
They and their children, and bowed to him.
Leah and her children approached him and bowed down.
Finally, Joseph and Rachel approached and bowed to him.
Impressed by the enormous size of Jacob's presents to him
He asked, "What was your reason for sending all this company
Of flocks which I met **on the way?"**

[1] To make the hindquarters of a cow edible for traditional Jews, the sciatic
nerve and other tendons and arteries must be removed. This costly procedure is
usually avoided. The hindquarters of the cow [filet mignon] are therefore not
eaten by Jews who fully observe the dietary laws.

He replied, "To please you, my lord."
Esau protested, "I have more than enough, my brother.
Keep what is yours." Jacob pleaded, "Do not refuse!
You will do me a kindness by accepting this present from me,
For in your face **of forgiveness** I have seen the face of God,
In that you accepted **me with a brother's love.**
Take **a small part of** my blessing which was brought to you.
Because the LORD was kind to me, I have everything."
Esau thought, "Yes, if he had not stolen my father's blessing,
God would have blessed me as he has blessed Jacob."
So when he pressed him **to accept the presents,** he took them.
Then, he proposed, "Let us travel together.
I will go ahead of you **to clear the way."**
Jacob declined, "My lord knows that the children are delicate,
Also the flocks and herds are nursing their young.
If we push them too hard even for one day, they could die.
Let my lord go **at his own speed** before his servant,
While I gradually lead my company at a speed
Compatible with the pace of the cattle and the children,
Until I come to my lord in his dwelling in Seir."
For Jacob thought, "If we travel together,
Esau may think again. He will remember what I did to him.
He will say, 'Why am I satisfied with his presents,
For could I not now take all that should have been mine!'"
Esau replied, "At least, let me leave some of my men
Who are with me **to protect you in the way that you go."**
Jacob would not have it. He said, "There is no need for this.
If I have won your favour, **allow us to travel on our own."**
Esau **was persuaded and** returned that day towards Seir.

Jacob, however, went towards Sukkoth, **and not to Seir.**
There he built himself a home and made booths for his cattle.
For this reason the place was called Sukkoth [booths].
Finally, Jacob arrived safely to the city of Shechem,
In the land of Canaan, after his return from Paddan-aram.
He encamped on the outskirts of the city.

On a piece of land he bought from the sons of
Hamor, Shechem's father, for a hundred pieces of silver
He set up his tents.
There he erected an altar to **confirm his ownership**
And called it El Elohai Yisrael.[1]

Give your daughter unto us.

Now Dinah, the daughter that Leah bore to Jacob,
Went out to meet the local girls.
Shechem, the son of Hamor, the local prince saw her.
He seized her, **and brought her to his house,**
Lay with her and dishonoured her.
He became passionate about Dinah, the daughter of Jacob,
He loved the girl and comforted her.
Shechem spoke to his father Hamor, insisting:
"Get me this girl to be my wife."
Jacob heard that he had defiled Dinah, his daughter.
His sons were with the cattle in the pasture.
Jacob decided to hold his peace until they came.
Hamor, the father of Shechem, came to Jacob to talk to him.
When the sons of Jacob returned from the pasture.
They heard what had happened to their sister
The men were distraught and very outraged
Over the vile act committed against the house of Israel:
To lie with a daughter of Jacob – an intolerable deed!

Hamor tried to placate them:
"Shechem, my son – his soul is tied to your daughter,
Give your permission for her to be his wife.
Make you marriages with our clan.
Give your daughters unto us
And take our daughters in marriage.
You will make your home with us.

[1] Meaning 'God, the God of Israel'.

The land will be yours to settle in,
To do business and to acquire holdings."

Shechem also begged her father and brothers.
"Let me win your approval.
Ask what you will of me and I will give it –
However great a dowry and presents.
Whatever you demand of me, I will agree.
Only give me the girl to be my wife."
The sons of Jacob answered Shechem and Hamor, his father,
With deceiving words because he had
Defiled Dinah, their sister: "We cannot allow this:
To give our sister to a man who is uncircumcised,
For that would cause us disgrace.
Only on these terms will we consent to your request,
To be as we are – every one of your males to be circumcised.
Then we will give our daughters to you
And take your daughters as our wives.
Then we will live with you and be one people.
But if you cannot consent to what we ask,
To be circumcised, we will take our daughter and be off."

Their words pleased Hamor and Shechem, the son of Hamor.
The lad did not waste any time in achieving this,
Because he longed for Jacob's daughter.
He was also the most honoured of all in his father's house.
Hamor and Shechem his son went to the city gate
To speak to the elders of their city. He said,
"These are men of integrity in their dealings with us.
Let them live in the land and do business in it,
The land is large enough for them too.
We will take their daughters to be our wives.
We will give our daughters to them.
But the men will only agree to live with us on this condition:
To be one people – if every male among us is circumcised
As they are circumcised. If we do this,
Will not their cattle, wealth and all their animals be ours?

Only let us agree so that they live with us."

All those who went out of the city gate **to fight in battle**
Agreed with Hamor and Shechem, his son.
Every male was circumcised which included
All those men able to leave the city **to engage in war.**
On the third day **after their circumcisions,**
When they were still hurting, two sons of Jacob,
Simeon and Levi, Dinah's brothers, each took his sword
And secretly came into the city and killed every man.
They slew Hamor and Shechem his son by the sword.
After they took Dinah from Shechem's house, they left.
When all the other sons of Jacob
Came to look on the slaughter,
They plundered the city for dishonouring their sister.
They seized their flocks, cattle and their donkeys,
Everything which was in the city and in the fields –
All their possessions.
They took captive their wives and children.
They looted everything in sight.

When he heard of what his sons had done
Jacob remonstrated with Simeon and Levi,
"You have made trouble for me by fouling my reputation
Among all the inhabitants – the Canaanites and the Perrizites.
Consider the consequences of what you have done.
I have so few men. **What is to prevent them?**
They will join together against me to attack me,
And I and my entire household will be destroyed!"
They replied: **"What would you have us do, our father?**
Should our sister have been treated as a whore?
The honour of our father's house will now be respected!"

Put away all the strange gods

Jacob was afraid of the evil that Simeon and Levi had done.
That night, he could not sleep for fear of his neighbours.
God appeared and said unto Jacob,
"Get you to Bethel. Live there and make an altar for the God
Who appeared to you when you fled from Esau, your brother."
Jacob said to his household, to all who were with him,
"Put away all the strange gods which you keep.
Purify yourselves and change your clothing.
We will rise and go up to Bethel.
I will make there an altar to the God
Who answered me in the day of my distress
Who stood by me in the journey I took."

The sons of Jacob were surprised by their father's command,
But they understood the danger of remaining in Shechem.
They agreed and they and their servants obeyed his word.
They gave to Jacob all the strange gods in their keeping.
Rachel too gave him the images she stole from her father,
And the rings **that were divine charms** from their ears
Jacob buried them under the terebinth by Shechem.
They **pulled up stakes and** began their departure.
A divine terror descended upon all the cities round about them
Because the sons of Jacob had destroyed the city of Shechem.
They did not **join together to** pursue after the sons of Jacob.

Jacob arrived at Luz which is in the land of Canaan –
[That is Bethel]. He and all the people that were with him.
There he built an altar and called the spot El Bethel,
The God of the House of God, because it was there that
The supreme God had appeared to him
When he escaped from his brother.
[**Now it was at that place that** Deborah, the nurse of Rebecca
Who also nursed Jacob as a child, died. **He grieved over her.**
She was buried below Bethel under an oak tree.
Because of his great sorrow, they named it 'Oak of Weeping'.]

At Bethel God appeared again to Jacob,
After his return from Paddan-aram to bless him.
He confirmed the blessings
He had promised on his flight from Esau
And when he fought with the Man of God.
God said to him the following, "Your name is Jacob.
No longer will your name be Jacob,
But you shall be called Israel."
[Thus his name became Israel]. God also told him,
"I am El Shaddai. Be fruitful and increase.
You will become not only a nation
But a community of nations.
Kings will come out of your loins.
The land which I promised Abraham and Isaac
I will give to you and to your descendants after you."
God left him in the place where he spoke to him –
The very place where God had spoken to him before,
Where Jacob had erected a pillar of stone, there
He had offered a drink offering and had poured oil over it.
Jacob had named the place where God spoke to him: Bethel.

After some time, they moved out of Bethel.
There was still some way before reaching Ephrath, and
Rachel went into labour and her pains were severe.
When she was in severe labour, the midwife told her,
"Do not be afraid, for now you will have another son."
As she breathed her last breath because she was dying,
She called him Benoni [son of my affliction].
But his father named him Benjamin [son of my right hand].
Thus Rachel died and was buried on the way to Ephrath,
That is Bethlehem. Jacob erected a pillar upon her grave.
It is the Pillar of Rachel's grave until this very day.
Jacob grieved over Rachel thirty days and thirty nights.

Israel, **for that was now his other name,** moved on and
Spread his encampment beyond the Tower of Eder.
It was not long after Israel dwelt in that area, that

Reuben went and slept with Bilhah, his father's concubine.
Israel heard **what he had done but said nothing.**

The sons of Jacob were twelve, in **the order of their mothers:**
The sons of Leah: Reuben, Jacob's first born, Simeon,
Levi and Judah and Issacher and Zebulun.
The sons of Rachel: Joseph and Benjamin.
The sons of Bilhah, Rachel's handmaid: Dan and Naphtali.
The sons of Zilpah, Leah's handmaid: Gad and Asher.
These are the sons of Jacob which were born to him in
Paddan-aram, **except for Benjamin, born in Bethlehem.**

Finally, Jacob came to Isaac, his father at Mamre –
To Kiryath-arba [that is Hebron]
Where Abraham and Isaac lived.
Isaac and Rebecca kissed their son and wept.
When they saw his sons and daughter, and his wealth.
They blessed God for he had guarded their son
And had fulfilled the blessing of Isaac upon him.
Isaac was one hundred and fifty-eight years old
When Jacob returned to him.
He lived to see the birth of grandsons,
And to comfort his son, Jacob, when Joseph was taken from him.

The years of Isaac's life were one hundred and eighty, when
Isaac surrendered his spirit and was gathered to his ancestors –
An old man fulfilled with length of days.
Esau and Jacob, his sons, buried him.

As to the generations of Esau who is Edom.
Esau had taken his wives of the daughters of Canaan:
Adah, bath[1] Elon the Hittite, and
Oholibamah, bath Anah, bath Zibeon the Hivite,
And Basemath, Ishmael's daughter, sister of Nebaioth.
Adah bore to Esau Eliphaz; Basemath bore Reuel and
Oholibamah bore Jeush and Jalam and Korah.

---

[1] 'bath' is Hebrew for 'daughter of' as 'ben' is for 'son of'.

These are the sons of Esau which were born unto him
In the land of Canaan. Esau took his wives, sons and daughters
And all the persons in his household and his cattle and
All his beasts and possessions which he had accumulated
In the land of Canaan, and went to another land
Away from his brother Jacob, for their substance
Was too great for them to dwell together.
For the land of their settlement could not sustain them both
Because of their livestock. So Esau dwelt on Mount Seir.
Esau is known as Edom. **All the generations of**
Esau, the names of their chieftains, the cities they ruled
Are recorded in the Books of the Genealogies?[1]

Then we will see what will become of his dreams

Jacob settled in the land of his father, in Canaan.
This is the history of Jacob.
Joseph was seventeen years old when
He was pasturing the flocks with his brothers:
He was a helping hand to the sons of Bilhah and
The sons of Zilpah, his father's concubines.
Joseph relayed their mischievous doings to their father.
He did not mind because Israel loved Joseph more than
All his sons because he was the child of his old age,
Also the son of his beloved wife, Rachel.
So he made him a **princely** coat which trailed down to his feet.
His brothers realized that their father loved him more than
All his brothers. So they hated him and never
Spoke a friendly word to him.

In spite of this, when Joseph dreamt a dream,
He told it to his brothers who **when they heard it**
Hated him even more. He said to them:

---

[1] See Appendix 4; for Genesis 36:9–43.

"Hear this dream which I have dreamt:
We are binding sheaves in the middle of the field
And notice – my sheaf stands upright, and
Your sheaves surround it and bow down to my sheaf."
His brothers retorted, "Do you intend to be king over us?
Do you mean to rule us?" So their hatred for him intensified
Because of his dreams and his words to them.

He dreamt another dream which he also told to his brothers.
He said: "Look, I had another dream, and in it
The sun, the moon and eleven stars are
Bowing down to me." He told it to his father
As well as to his brothers. His father berated him,
With these words, "What kind of dream is this that
You have dreamt? Shall I, your mother and brothers
Come and prostrate ourselves to the ground before you!"
So his brothers were jealous of him,
But his father kept this in mind.

His brothers went to pasture their father's flocks in Shechem.
Israel said to Joseph, "Are your brothers
Not pasturing in Shechem?
Come. I will send you to them." He replied, "Here I am."
He thought, "Why is my father sending me such a long way
To my brothers when he knows how much they hate me?"
He then said to him, "Go, see how your brothers fare?
And bring me back word of the cattle."
For Jacob thought: "When my sons see that I have sent Joseph,
They will know that I love them too, and will forgive him."
He sent him off from the Vale of Hebron
And he reached Shechem.[1]

---

[1] Why Jacob should send Joseph, and not other servants, a distance of some fifty to sixty miles to enquire after the welfare of his other sons beggars the imagination. I have inserted an explanation which does not really satisfy me. Perhaps, despite its implausibility, this is the only way for the author to weave his great moral tale of sin, remorse and repentance and to bring the Israelites down into Egypt in preparation for their divine redemption.

A man found him lost and wandering in the steppes **of Shechem.**
The man asked him, "What are you looking for?"
He replied, "I am looking for my brothers.
Tell me, where are they pasturing?"
The man answered, "They have left this place
But I heard them saying. Let us go to Dothan."
Joseph went after his brothers, and found them in Dothan.

They saw him coming from afar, and before he reached them
They conspired against him to kill him.
One said to the other, "This dreamer of ours is coming.
Come now let us kill him and throw him into one of the pits.
We will say, 'A vicious beast ate him.'
Then we will see what will come of his dreams!"
Reuben, **the firstborn,** heard them and saved him from them.
For he said, "Let us not destroy a life." Reuben argued
With them, "Do not spill his blood, throw him into that pit
In the wilderness, but do not lay a hand upon him."
He intended to save him from their hands,
To return him to his father.

When Joseph reached his brothers, **he was there a moment**
When they stripped Joseph of his coat; yes, the princely coat
Which trailed down to his feet, took him and
Threw him into a pit – the pit was desolate, without water.
They left Joseph shouting and sobbing in the pit.
They went off not to hear his cries.
After pasturing their flocks, they sat down for their meal.
When they looked up they saw **at a great distance**
A caravan **probably** of Ishmaelites coming from Gilead,
With their camels, **no doubt** bearing spices, balm and myrrh
To bring and sell in Egypt. Judah said to his brothers,[1]

---

[1] Many students of Genesis believe that there are two stories intertwined here. One in which Reuben intends to save Joseph but is thwarted by the Midianites. Another that it is Judah who takes on the role of saviour by selling him to the Ishmaelites. Later in the story it is Reuben and Judah who compete to persuade Jacob to allow them to take Benjamin down to Egypt.

"What use is there in killing our brother and hiding our crime
After we have left him to die in the pit without food?
Let us sell him to the Ishmaelites
Without laying our hands on him
Because he is our brother, our own flesh." His brothers agreed.
After the meal, they rested themselves and slept.
From the other direction, Midianite merchants were passing.
They heard the cries of Joseph. They drew and lifted
Joseph from the pit. **While he pleaded to be released**
They sold Joseph to the Ishmaelites **who had come upon them,**
For twenty pieces of silver. They took Joseph to Egypt.
Reuben **awoke and** returned to the pit **to save him.**
To his horror, Joseph was not in the pit.
He tore his clothes in grief and returned to his brothers,
Shrieking, "The boy is not there; where shall I flee
From my father's woe, for I will be held accountable!"
Judah comforted Reuben, "Joseph must still be alive.
While we slept, the Ishmaelites must have found him.
They will take him to Egypt to sell him into slavery."
But Reuben cried out: "Is not Ishmael our father's uncle?
Are they not our kinsmen and will not our father know
What we have done to our brother?"
The brothers said to him, "They will not tell him
For it is not done to sell a kinsman into slavery.
They will keep it a secret as we too will hide our sin."

They took Joseph's coat and slaughtered a he-goat
And dipped the coat in its blood; they sent the princely coat
With servants; they did not wish to witness Jacob's grief.
The servants brought it to their father, saying,
According to their masters' instructions, "We have found this.
Do you recognize it as your son's coat or is it not?"
He recognized it; he cried,
"My son's coat.
A vicious beast has eaten him!
Torn, torn is Joseph."

Jacob rent his clothes and put sackcloth on his loins.
He mourned for his son many many days.
His sons and daughters, **his grandchildren,**
Tried to comfort him but he refused to be comforted,
For he said, "I will go down to Sheol
To my son, mourning." Thus his father wept for him.
But, **because of the sale of** the Midianites,
The Ishmaelites sold him in Egypt
To Potiphar, an officer of Pharaoh's, his chief steward.

Let her be burnt

During that time, **before Joseph was sold into Egypt,**
Judah left his family and lived with an Adullamite,
His name was Hirah.
There Judah saw a daughter of a Canaanite,
Whose name was Shua. He took her and lay with her.
She conceived and bore him a son. He named him Er.
She conceived again and bore him a second son.
He named him Onan. Yet again she bore him a son.
He named him Shelah. He was at Chezib when she bore him.

Many years later his elder sons reached manhood
[Joseph had been sold into slavery]. Judah took a wife for
Er, his firstborn, whose name was Tamar.
Er, Judah's firstborn, was wicked in the sight of the LORD.
And the LORD caused him to die.
Judah said to Onan, "Go unto your brother's widow.
Do your duty by her as a brother-in-law.[1]
And raise up descendants in your brother's name."
Onan knew that the child would not be counted as his

[1] In order to maintain the name and 'immortality' of a deceased person without any child; also to give the deceased through his child an inheritance, from which the mother could draw income, the brother-in-law had the obligation to give the widow a child. When there was no brother-in-law, this obligation was extended to the closest relative.

And that part of his father's inheritance would go to him.
When he lay with his brother's wife
He withdrew from her and spilt himself on the ground
So as not to provide a descendant to his brother.
What he did was evil in the sight of the LORD
And he also caused him to die.
Judah said to Tamar, his daughter-in-law,
"Stay as a widow in your father's house
Until Shelah my son is grown, **then I will give him to you.**"
But thought, "In case he too will die as did his brothers."
Tamar departed and settled in her father's house.

Years passed, and the daughter of Shua, Judah's wife, died.
Judah was comforted **and ceased to mourn over her.**
He went to join his sheep-shearers, at Timnah,
He and his friend Hirah the Adullamite.
Tamar was told, "Look, your father-in-law is
Going up to Timnah to shear his flocks."
She took off her widow's rags, covered herself with a veil,
Covered herself completely and sat by the crossroads,
Which was on the way towards Timnah,
Because she knew that
Shelah had grown up but she had not been
Given to him as his wife.

When Judah saw her, he thought she was a whore
For she had covered her face. He turned to her by the road,
And said, "Let me sleep with you," because he did not know
She was his daughter-in-law. She asked, "What will you pay
Me for having intercourse with you?" He replied,
"I will send you a kid of the goats." She agreed,
"Only if you give me some security until you send it."
He asked, "What security shall I give you?"
She said, "Your seal and sash and the staff you carry."
He gave these to her, went into her and she conceived by him.
She got up, returned home, removed her veil
And dressed herself in her widow's rags.

Judah sent a kid of the goats by his friend
The Adullamite and to retrieve the security from the woman.
But he could not find her. He enquired of the locals,
Asking, "Where is the whore who sat by the crossroads?"
They answered, "There was no whore **such as you describe.**"
He returned to Judah and told him, "I could not find her;
And the local men say that there never was such a whore."
Judah responded, "Let her have them: **the signet and staff.**
The alternative is to make fools of ourselves.
I did the honourable thing. I sent the kid
But you could not find her."

Three months later, Judah was told these words,
"Tamar, your daughter-in-law, has behaved like a whore.
She has conceived through whoring.
As an adulteress she deserves to be burnt."[1]
Judah was pleased because he thought,
"Now I will not need to give her to my son, Shelah."
So he had no compassion for her; Judah ordered,
"Bring her our and let her be burnt!"
When she was brought out **of her father's house**
She sent word to her father-in-law.
"By the man who owns these am I pregnant;
Recognize to whom this seal, sash and staff belong."
Judah recognized them and confessed.
"She is more righteous than I
For I did not give her to Shelah."
But he did not sleep with her again.

At the time of her labour, there were twins in her belly.
As she began to give birth, one put forth a hand.
The midwife took a scarlet thread and bound it on his finger,
To signify, "This child was born first." But it happened
That as he drew his hand back, his brother came out.

---

[1] Tamar was still considered as Er's wife until she was released from her
obligation to have a child through her deceased husband's brother.

Laughing, she said,
"How did you make a breach for yourself?"
He was called Perez [to breach].
Afterward his brother came out.
He was named Zerah [to shine].

His master's wife raised her eyes to Joseph

Now Joseph had been brought down to Egypt.
Potiphar, an official of Pharaoh's, his Chief Steward
And an Egyptian,[1]
Bought him from the Ishmaelites
Who had brought him there.
The LORD was with Joseph and he was a success.
He stayed in the Egyptian's, his master's, house.
His master saw that the LORD was with him
Because the LORD prospered all that he set his hand to.
Joseph pleased him and personally served him.
Eventually, he appointed him to supervise his household.
All that he owned, he entrusted to him.

From the time he appointed him over his household,
And charged him with all that he owned,
The LORD blessed the Egyptian's household because of Joseph.
The blessing of the LORD was upon everything he owned
Both in his house and on his farms,
He left everything in the hands of Joseph.
He concerned himself with nothing, only the food he ate.
Joseph was a handsome man and charismatic.

It was after these events – **the promotion of Joseph** –
That his master's wife raised her eyes to Joseph.
She said to him, "Sleep with me."

[1] That Genesis should describe Potiphar as an Egyptian would seem to indicate that the author wishes to set the story at the time when the Hyksos, Bedouin Semites, were ruling Egypt. Potiphar's position at court would therefore have been exceptional and worth noting.

But he protested. He said to his master's wife,
"Having me here, my master knows
Nothing of what happens in the house,
Everything he possesses he entrusts to my stewardship.
He is not greater in this house than I.
He has withheld nothing from me, except for you,
In that you are his wife. **Much as I might like to,**
How could I do such a wicked thing and sin against God!"

But much as she harassed Joseph day by day,
He did not obey her, to lie next to her or to be with her.
On one such a day, he entered the house to do his work.
None of the menservants were inside the house.
She grabbed his coat and said, "Lie with me."
He fled and came outside but left his cloak in her hands.
When she saw that he left his cloak in her hands
To flee and go outside, she called to the household servants
And said to them these **lying** words, "See, he has brought in
A Hebrew to make fools of us. He came to sleep with me.
But I screamed in a loud voice.
When he heard that I raised my voice, calling for help,
He left his cloak as he ran outside."
She kept the garment by him until Joseph's master came home.
She told him these very same words,
"The Hebrew slave whom you brought us came in to me
To make a plaything of me, but when I raised my voice
And cried, he left his cloak by me as he ran outside."

When his master heard his wife's story which she told him:
Such and such your slave did to me, he became furious.
Joseph did not seek to defend himself,
For how could his master admit
That it was his wife who asked him to sleep with her.
Joseph's master had him seized and put in prison,
The place where the king's prisoners were bound over.
There he remained in prison, but the LORD was with Joseph
And showed him kindness and enabled him

To win the favour of the prison's governor. So much so,
That the governor handed over to Joseph the supervision
Of all those who were confined in the prison.
For all that was done there, he was responsible.
The prison governor never checked anything he did,
Because the LORD was with him.
Whatever he did, the LORD made it prosper.

After a time, the head wine steward and the
Head of the bakery
Were thought to have sinned against their master,
The king of Egypt.
Pharaoh was incensed against his two officials,
Against his steward of the wines and steward of the bakery.
He put them in custody in the prison of the head steward,[1]
The place where Joseph was confined.
The head steward appointed Joseph to be with them.
He ministered to them and they were in his custody for a year,
The time when Pharaoh would decide the fate of each of them.

Both of them dreamt a dream, each one his own,
On the same night, each with its own meaning:
The head wine steward and the head of the bakery
Of the king of Egypt who were confined in the prison.
Joseph came to them in the morning and they were distraught.
He asked the officials of Pharaoh who were with him
In custody in his master's house: "Why are you so sad today?"
They replied, "We dreamt a dream and there is no one to
Interpret them." Joseph said to them, "Interpretations are God's.
Tell them to me, **perhaps God will tell me their meaning."**
The head wine steward recounted his dream to Joseph.
"A vine is before me. The vine has three branches.

---

[1] Potiphar, Joseph's master, is entitled as head steward. If this is the same man, it would appear that Potiphar had his own prison for VIP criminals and suspects. His appointment of Joseph to serve them may indicate that the author wishes to suggest that Potiphar came to believe in his innocence in regard to his wife's accusation.

They had just budded but their flowers burst forth.
In an instant its clusters ripened into grapes.
Pharaoh's cup was in my hand and I took the grapes.
I pressed them into Pharaoh's cup and
Put the cup into the palm of Pharaoh's hand."

Now Joseph knew that the head wine steward and
The head of the bakeries were suspected of poisoning Pharaoh,
For he had become ill after eating dinner.
When Joseph heard this dream, he knew that
The head wine steward was innocent
Because he was giving wine to Pharaoh.
Pharaoh would find out that he was a man of integrity,
A loyal servant and return him to his house.

Joseph said, "This is its interpretation.
The three branches are three days.
In three days, Pharaoh will lift up your head
And restore you to your office.
You will place Pharaoh's cup into his hand,
As was the custom when you were his wine steward.
But keep me in your mind when all is well with you again,
Do me a kindness. Recommend me to Pharaoh,
Bring me out of this prison-house.
For I was abducted out of the land of the Hebrews.
Also, I did nothing wrong here
For which to be placed in this dungeon."

When the head steward of the bakery
Heard the good interpretation,
He was eager to recount his own dream. He told Joseph,
"I was also in my dream, and three white wicker baskets
Are on my head. On the uppermost basket there were
All kinds of dishes for Pharaoh made by the bakers.
But the birds were eating them from on the top of my head."
Joseph understood from the dream that he was guilty
For he was not giving his food to Pharaoh but to scavengers.

Joseph answered him, "This is its interpretation.
The three baskets are three days.
In three days, Pharaoh will remove your head from you.
You will be hung on a tree and birds will eat your flesh."

It was on the third day, Pharaoh's birthday,
When he would decide whom to favour
And whom to condemn.
He made a feast for all his ministers. Then
He, **so to speak**, lifted up the heads of his head wine steward
And head steward of the bakery before his ministers:
He restored the wine steward to his former office so
He could hold his head up high to hand
The cup into Pharaoh's hand.
But as to the steward of the bakeries, he hanged him.
But only after he had lifted his head from off his body
Just as Joseph had interpreted to both of them.
The wine steward did not remember Joseph's plea,
He completely forgot him **when he was restored to his office.**

Where will we find a man such as this?

Two years later, **when Joseph was thirty years old**
And had been in Egypt for thirteen years,
Pharaoh had a dream; he was standing by the Nile.
Out of the river emerged seven cows – sleek and plump.
They were grazing in the reed grass by the river.
And, behold, seven other cows emerged after them
From the Nile – thin and sickly.
They stood by the other cows at the river's edge.
The seven sickly and emaciated cows ate
The seven sleek and plump cows. Pharaoh woke up.

He slept and had another dream. See –
Seven ears of grain grew out of one stalk – healthy and ripe.
Seven thin grains scorched by the east wind
Sprouted up after them. The seven thin ears of grain

Swallowed up the seven healthy and ripe ears of grain.
Pharaoh woke up and, it was only a dream!

That morning his heart beat quickly; he sent to call for
All the magicians of Egypt and all its wise men.
Pharaoh recounted his dreams but none interpreted them
To Pharaoh's satisfaction. And the head wine steward
Said to Pharaoh, "I remember my sins today.
Pharaoh was angry with his ministers.
He placed me in custody in the house of the head steward,
Me and the head steward of the bakeries.
We dreamt a dream one night, I and he,
Each of us dreaming a dream with a special meaning.
There was in our attendance a Hebrew lad,
The head steward's slave. We recounted them.
He interpreted our dreams for us,
Telling each of us the meaning of his dream.
As he interpreted them, so it was!
I was restored to my office and he was hanged."

Pharaoh sent to call for Joseph. With great haste
They rushed him out of the dungeon. He shaved and
Changed his clothes and came before Pharaoh.
Pharaoh told Joseph. "I have dreamt two dreams and
There has been no satisfactory interpretation of them.
I have heard this about you that when
You hear a dream, you are able to interpret it."
Joseph replied to Pharaoh, "Not I, my lord, but
God will respond to Pharaoh's benefit."
Pharaoh recounted his dreams to Joseph,
"In my dream I am standing by the edge of the Nile
Behold seven cows – sleek and plump –
Rise out of the Nile and pasture among the reed grass.
Behold seven other cows, thin and sickly, emerge after them.
I have never experienced in all of Egypt
Such sickly looking creatures as these.
The thin and sickly cows ate the first healthy cows.

When they were eaten by them, you would not have known
That this had happened because they looked as
Sickly as they had at first. I awoke in shock!
I saw in the second dream seven ears of grain growing
Out of one stalk – thick and luxuriant. And behold!
Seven more ears of grains – withered and thin, as though
Smitten by an east wind sprout up after them.
The seven weather-beaten ears of grain
Ate the seven luxuriant ears of grain **and**
They too looked no different than before.
I have put this to my magicians who can tell me nothing."

Joseph said to Pharaoh, "The dreams of Pharaoh are as one.
What God is about to do, he has told Pharaoh.
The seven plump cows are seven years.
The seven healthy ears of grain are seven years.
They are one dream **with one meaning.**
The thin and sickly cows who arose after them
Are seven years.
The seven seedless ears of grain smitten by an east wind,
These represent seven years of famine.
This is what I intimated earlier to Pharaoh:
What God is about to do he has shown to Pharaoh.
Seven years of great plenty are coming to the whole of Egypt.
After them will come seven years of famine;
Those of great plenty will be forgotten in the land of Egypt
Because the famine will eat up the land.
The years of plenty will not even be remembered
Because the famine afterwards will be so severe.
As to the reason for Pharaoh having two dreams
With the same meaning, it is to reinforce that the word truly
Comes from God who hastens to fulfil it."

Now, **if I may presume to advise Pharaoh,**
Let Pharaoh look for a man of good judgement and wise
And set him over the land of Egypt. Let Pharaoh do this.
Let this man appoint commissars over the land

To collect twenty percent of the land's harvest
In taxes during the seven years of plenty.
They will gather all the produce of the good years to come
And store up the grain under Pharaoh's authority
For food in the cities and let them keep guard over it.
The stores of food will be a security for the land during
The seven years of famine which will befall the land of Egypt,
So that the land will not be wiped out by the famine.

Joseph was dismissed and waited in the anteroom.
The advice of Joseph pleased Pharaoh and his ministers.
Pharaoh asked his ministers: "Where will we find a man
Such as this – a man in whom is the inspiration of God?"
They agreed with Pharaoh and sent for Joseph.
Pharaoh said to Joseph, "In as much as God has informed you
Of all this, there can be no one more competent,
Wise and of greater judgement than yourself.
You will be over my household.
By your command will my people be ruled.
Only by virtue of the throne am I greater than you."
Pharaoh went on to say to Joseph,
"See, I have set you over the entire land of Egypt."
Pharaoh took the signet ring off his hand,
He put it on the hand of Joseph and clothed him in
Garments of fine linen and placed a gold chain on his neck.
He was driven in his second-best chariot.
They ordered all to bow before him.
He was appointed **as viceroy** over the entire land of Egypt
For Pharaoh had said to Joseph, "While I am still Pharaoh
Without your leave no man will raise a hand
Or a foot in the whole land of Egypt."
Pharaoh renamed Joseph Zaphenath-paneah.[1]
He gave him a wife: Asenath the daughter of Poti-phera,
The priest of On. So Joseph went out over the land of Egypt.

---

[1] English meaning is "Food man of Egypt".

Joseph was thirty years old when he stood before
Pharaoh, king of Egypt. Joseph left Pharaoh's presence
To survey the entire land of Egypt.
In the seven years of plenty the earth yielded in abundance.
For seven years he gathered up all
The food owed to the Pharaoh
In the land of Egypt. He stored the food in the towns,
Putting in each the food grown in the outlying countryside.
Joseph gathered the grain, like the sands of the sea,
In great abundance; so much that he stopped counting,
For there were not enough numbers.

The ministers of Pharaoh complained,
"Let the food be in the capital
Where the army can guard it."
Pharaoh sent for Joseph and asked, "What are you doing?"
Who will protect the grain in the distant towns?"
Joseph answered, "If it please my lord, the famine will become
Severe and the people will forget the years of plenty
When they should have stored up food. Instead they sold it
For silver and gold because they thought
They would never lack food.
When they are hungry, if all the food is in the capital
There will be a great uprising. They will come to your palace
To demand bread. No army will be able to control them.
See, I have stored the food in all their towns and
Appointed their kinsmen as officials in charge of the food.
When they have no food, they will go to them.
They will buy food for their silver, their gold and jewels,
For their land and their very lives, but they will not rebel.
Because it is their kinsmen who will act for Pharaoh.
Besides, my lord, the city of Pharaoh could not contain
The grain because of its multitude beyond measure,
Nor are there enough oxen and carts to carry them here."
Pharaoh replied, "You are wise. Do as you will."

To Joseph were born two sons before the famine years;

Who were born to him by Asenath the daughter of Poti-phera,
The priest of On. Joseph named the first born Menasseh
Because, "God has made me forget [*nasani*] all my hardships
And **the suffering caused me by** my father's house."
The second son he named Ephraim because, "God
Has made me fruitful [*hiphrani*] in the land of my affliction."

The seven years of plenty in the land of Egypt ended
Just as Joseph had said. And there was famine in all
The lands of the earth but in Egypt there was bread.
When the individual stores of bread were used up
The land of Egypt became affected by the famine,
The people cried out to Pharaoh for bread.
Pharaoh made a proclamation to all the Egyptians:
Go to Joseph and act according to his instructions.
The famine was over the whole world.
Then Joseph opened up all the store houses and
Sold grain to the Egyptians. The famine intensified in Egypt.
The whole earth came to Egypt to buy grain from Joseph
Because the famine had become fierce in all of the earth.

We are sons of one man, we are honest men

Jacob knew that there was grain in Egypt.
He said to his sons, "Why do you keep staring at each other?
I hear that there is grain in Egypt. Go down there.
Buy grain from there so that we may live and not die."
Ten of Joseph's brothers went down to buy grain from Egypt.
But Benjamin, Joseph's brother, Jacob did not send,
For he thought, "Lest an accident occur to him,
As it did to Joseph when I sent him to see his brothers."

The sons of Israel who came to buy grain were
Among all the other foreigners coming to Egypt because
The famine was very severe in the land of Canaan.

Joseph knew that his father's house would need food,
So, being the Governor over the whole country
Joseph was the one who sold grain to all purchasers
From all the foreign lands. When Joseph's brothers arrived,
They bowed themselves down with their faces to the ground.
Joseph looked at his brothers and recognized them,
But he remained aloof from them and
Spoke harsh words to them. He asked them,
"Where do you come from?" They replied,
"From the land of Canaan to buy food."
While Joseph recognized his brothers,
Because of his beard and royal apparel,
They did not recognize him.
Joseph remembered the dreams
Which he had dreamt about them,
How their sheaves and stars had bowed down to him.

Joseph said to them, "You are spies,
You have come to see the vulnerability of our borders
So that your countrymen may invade us and take our food."
They protested as one to him, "No, my lord.
Your servants have only come to purchase food.
We are all sons of one man. We are honest men.
Your servants were never spies." But he persisted,
"No! You have come to assess the vulnerability of the land."
To defend themselves, they explained their background.
They said, "Your servants – we are twelve brothers,
The sons of one man in the land of Canaan.
The youngest remains now with our father.
The other is no longer . . ."
Joseph retorted, "It is as I have said to you, you are spies!
But this is how you can vindicate yourselves,
By the life of Pharaoh, by no other way can
You clear yourselves from this accusation.
Only if your younger brother comes here.
Send one of you to bring your brother.

You, who remain, will be imprisoned
So that your words may be tested.
Are you telling the truth? If not, by Pharaoh's life,
You are spies." He put them together in a cell for three days.

While they were in prison, they cried out to God,
"Deliver us for our father's sake.
Unless we bring him food,
He and all that belongs to him will die."
They quarrelled among themselves as to
Who should go to fetch Benjamin.
Reuben said, "I must go for I am the first born."
But the others said, "No, you will not persuade our father
To let Benjamin go with you since you slept with Zilpah."
Simeon, the second born, said, "I will go then."
The brothers said, "Our father is angry with you and Levi
Because of what you did in the city of Shechem,
When you made him unwelcome to the dwellers in the land.
We will send Judah. Perhaps our father will listen to him."
When they were summoned out of prison, on the third day,
Joseph said to them, "Do this so that you may live,
Because I fear God, **I have changed my mind.**
To see whether you are honest men, only one of your kinsmen
Will be locked up in prison. As to the rest of you, go
Take grain to keep starvation from your homes.
But you must bring your youngest brother to me,
To verify your words, so that you will not die of famine."

They nodded assent. But they murmured to each other,
"While we are not spies we are guilty because of our brother.
We saw his great suffering and when he begged us
We took no notice. On this account has
This suffering happened to us." Reuben chided them,
"Ah, did I not say to you, 'Do not sin against the boy!'
But you did not listen, and his blood is required of us."
They could not know that Joseph heard and understood
Because an interpreter stood between them.

He turned away from them and wept. **He thought,**
"They are beginning to feel remorse for what they have done."
He could not hold back his tears for he pitied them.
He returned to them and spoke to them.
He took Simeon from them **because he thought,**
"Simeon and Levi make trouble together. I will divide them."
He had him bound before them **and taken away.**

Joseph gave orders regarding his brothers, to fill their bags,
To return their money, each in his own sack, and
To provide them with food for the journey.
This they did for them. They loaded their donkeys with grain,
And went off from there. One of them opened his sack to give
Fodder to his donkey at an inn. He saw his money,
It was at the very top of his sack. He shouted to his brothers,
"My money has been returned. See, it is in my sack."
Their hearts stopped. Anxiously, they looked at each other,
"What is God doing to us? **If the man thought we were spies,**
Why has he returned our money?

They came to Jacob in the land of Canaan.
They recounted all that had happened to them.
"The man, the lord of the country, spoke harshly to us.
He thought we had come to spy out the land.
We said to him, 'We are honest men, not spies.
We are twelve brothers, the sons of one father;
One is no longer with us and the youngest is now with
Our father in the land of Canaan.' The man, lord of the land,
Said to us, 'By this will I know if you are honest.
Leave one of your brothers with me and take grain
To prevent starvation in your homes and go on your way,
But bring your youngest brother to me.
Then will I know that you are not spies, but honest men.
I will return your brother and you can trade in the land.'"

When they were emptying their sacks, everyone's
Money purse was in his sack. When they saw their

Packets of money, they and their father were aghast.
The anxiety was too much for their father.
Jacob, their father, cried out to them,
"You are robbing me of my children. Joseph is no more.
Simeon is also gone. And now you want to take Benjamin.
All this has come upon me. **I cannot cope with it.**"
Reuben, to reassure him, said to his father:
"You may kill my two sons if I do not bring him back to you.
Entrust him to me. I will bring him back to you."
He **threw up his hands in despair and** said,
"Will the death of two more sons, for are yours not mine,
Comfort me! My son will not go down with you.
His brother is dead! Only he remains **from his mother**.
Were any mischief to happen to him on the road you take,
You would bring down my heavy head with grief to Sheol[1]."

The famine remained severe in the country

The famine was devastating the land.
When they finished eating the grain they brought from Egypt,
Their father said to them, "Return to Egypt,
Buy us some food." Judah said to him,
"The man swore, warning us against coming before him,
'Unless your brother is with you.' If you send
Our brother with us, we will go down and buy food.
But if you do not send him, we will not go down,
For the man said to us, **again and again and again,**
'You will not see my face unless your brother is with you.'"
Jacob moaned, "Why have you caused me such trouble,
By telling the man that you had another brother?"
They answered, "The man persisted in asking us
About our family situation, like, 'Is your father still alive?

---

[1] The Biblical equivalent to the Greek Hades, the nether world.

Do you have other brothers?' We responded appropriately.
How could we have known that he would say,
'Bring down your brother'?" Judah said to Israel, his father,
"Send the lad with me, let us set off
So that we may live and not die.
Not only us, even you and our little ones.
I will be his guarantor.
I will be answerable to you for him.
If I do not bring him to you
And place him before you.
If I do not do this my guilt will
Last as long as the days we both live.
For if we had not spent so much time dithering,
We could have been there and back twice."
Israel, their father, said to them,
"If it must be so, then do this:
Put the delicacies of our land into your bags.
Bring the man presents, some balm, some honey,
Spices and myrrh, pistachios and almonds.
Take double the money in your hands
To make up for the money which was in your sacks.
Return it with your own hands; maybe it was only an error.
And take your brother. Get up and return to the man!
Let God Shaddai see that you find compassion
Before the man that he may release your other
Brother to you as well as my Benjamin.
If I am bereft of my children, I am bereft!"

The men took these presents; they took double the money
And Benjamin, and made their way down to Egypt.
They stood before Joseph's storerooms,
When Joseph saw that Benjamin was with them,
He did not acknowledge them but said to his house steward,
"Take the men to my home, slaughter and prepare meat,
Because the men will eat with me at noon."
The man did as Joseph had instructed him and

Brought the men to Joseph's palace.
The men were frightened when they were taken to
Joseph's palace, for they thought, "It is because of the money
Which was returned to our sacks during the first trip.
We have been brought here for him to turn against us.
He will use this as an excuse to attack us
And take us as slaves and to confiscate our donkeys –
Indeed all our possessions. He does this at home,
So that he may enrich himself and not Pharaoh."
With this in mind, they approached the man in charge of
Joseph's house and they spoke to him in the courtyard.
They said, "Please, my lord, we came down originally
To buy food. When **on our return home** we came to an inn,
Opened our bags and saw **to our surprise**
Our silver of the same weight **which we brought**
Down with us to purchase food was in every man's bag.
With our very hands we have brought the money back.
We have brought more money to buy food.
We do not know how the money
Came to be in our bags." He assured them,
"It is well with you. Do not fret.
Your God and the God of your father
Must have put the treasure with your bags.
I had your money."
With that, he brought Simeon out to them.
Then the man brought the men into Joseph's home.
He placed water before them to wash their feet,
And fodder for their donkeys.

They prepared the gifts when Joseph arrived at noon,
Because they heard that he would break bread there.
When Joseph arrived home, they brought him the presents
Which were with them into the house
And bowed down to him to the very ground.
He was most courteous. He asked how they were,
"Is your aged father of whom you spoke still alive?"

They said, "Your servant, our father, is well and still lives."
Again they bowed to him and offered homage.
He looked up and saw Benjamin, his brother,
His mother's son, and asked, "Is this then
Your youngest brother of whom you spoke?"
He said to him, "God be gracious to you, my son."
Joseph rushed **to end the meeting** because his heart
Yearned for his brother. He needed to weep **privately**
Because the time had not come to reveal who he was.
He entered his private chamber and there he wept.
He washed his face, went out and took control of himself.

He said, "Serve the food." He sat alone,
They too sat separately. The Egyptians who were eating
With him also sat separately because
Egyptians were not able to eat with Hebrews because
This would have been a defilement for them.
They were sitting before him **according to his seating plan,**
The eldest first, the rest according to age until the youngest.
The men expressed amazement to each other **at his knowledge.**
Portions of food were taken to them from where he sat.
Benjamin's portion was five times more than that of the others.
They drank and got drunk with him.

He ordered the house steward as follows:
"Fill the men's sacks with food, as much as they can hold.
Put everyone's money on the top part of the sack.
My silver cup, put in the top of the sack of the youngest,
Together with his money brought to purchase grain."
He did just as Joseph had ordered.
At morning light, **with happy hearts for Benjamin was safe**
And Simeon released from bondage, they were sent off,
They, their donkeys and carts. When they were out of the city,
But not far away, Joseph ordered his steward,
"Go after the men and, when you overtake them, say to them,
'Why have you rewarded my kindnesses
To you with wickedness?

Is this cup which you have stolen not the cup from which
My lord drinks and from which he sees into the future?
You have behaved most wickedly in what you have done.'''
He overtook them and spoke these words to them.
In disbelief they said to him, "Why does our lord say this?
God forbid that your servants would do such a thing.
The money we found in our sacks we brought back from
The land of Canaan. How could you imagine that we would
Steal from your master's house silver or gold!
Let the person with whom it is found die
And we too will become my lord's slaves,
So certain are we of our total innocence."
He said to them, "Let it be as you say, but only
The person with whom it is found will be my slave.
You others are innocent **and not to be punished."**
The men quickly unloaded the sacks from the carts
Onto the ground and each one opened his sack.
They began the search with the oldest down to the youngest.
The cup was discovered in Benjamin's sack.
With uncontrollable grief, they tore at their clothes,
Loaded every man his donkey and cart and
Returned to the city.
Judah, **the guarantor for Benjamin's safety,**
And his brothers arrived at Joseph's palace.
He was still there. They prostrated themselves before him
To the ground. Joseph said to them, "What deed is this
That you have done? Do you not know that men
Such as I can see into the future **and**
Know the truths and lies in human hearts?"
Judah knew that it would be no use to defend themselves.
It was not the matter of the stolen cup from the man
But because of what they had done to Jacob
In stealing Joseph from him and their cruelty to him.
Now, for this sin, he would have to return without Benjamin
And be cursed forever. So Judah said,
"What can we say to my master?

With what can we plead?
How can we be vindicated?
God has discovered your servants' sin.
We will be servants to my master,
We and the one in whose possession the cup was found."
For Judah and the brothers did not want to return to Jacob,
To witness his grief when Benjamin was not with them.
But he rejected this, "God forbid that I should do this.
Only the man with whom the cup was found,
He will be my slave. You may go up in peace to your father."

I am Joseph. Is my father still alive?

Judah went close to him and said, "Please, my lord,
Allow your servant to speak quietly into my master's ear.
Let him not be angry with your servant,
Because you are as Pharaoh.
Remember when you asked your servants,
'Do you have a father or brother?'
We replied to my master, 'We have an elderly father
And a brother, a child he had when he was old.
His brother died and he alone remains from his mother.
She died when she gave birth to him. His father adores him.
You said to your servants, 'Bring him down to me
So that I may look at him. We said to my lord,
The lad cannot leave his father,
For if he left his father, his father would die.
But you insisted with your servants,
'If your younger brother does not come down with you,
You will not see my face again.'
So when we went up to your servant, our father,
We told him the words of my lord.
After a time our father instructed us: 'Go buy us some food.'
We said, 'We cannot go down
Unless our younger brother is with us.
Only then can we go down because

We cannot see the face of the man
If our youngest brother is not with us.'
Your servant, my father, said to me,
'You know that my wife bore two sons to me.
One of them left me, and I said, surely
He has been savaged by wild beasts.
I have not seen him since.
If you now take this son from me, and an
Accident befalls him, you will bring down
My hoary head to Sheol.'
Now, if I return to your servant, my father,
The lad not being with us –
He whose life is bound up with his life –
And he sees that the lad is not with us,
He will die, and your servants
Will have brought down the hoary head
Of your servant, my father, with grief to Sheol.
Also, your servant made himself a guarantor for the lad
To his father for I said, If I do not bring him back to you,
I will have sinned against my father all my life.
Now let your servant be my lord's slave
Instead of the lad and allow him to go up with his brothers.
For how shall I go up to my father
Lest I see the evil that will strike my father
When he sees that the lad is not with me?"

Joseph could not contain his emotions
Before all who stood by him.
He called out, "Send everyone away."
No one stood by him when
He made himself known to his brothers,
He wept so loudly that all
The Egyptians heard, the house of Pharaoh heard!
"I am Joseph. Is my father still alive!"
His brothers could not answer him,
So shocked were they by his presence.

Joseph said to his brothers, "Come close to me, please."
They came closer. He repeated, "I am Joseph, your brother,
Whom you sold to Egypt.
Do not be upset or angry with yourselves
For causing me to be sold to this place,
For to preserve our lives did God send me before you.
For two years now the famine has been in the country.
There will be a further five years
With neither sowing nor harvesting.
God sent me before you to maintain your offspring on earth,
To keep you alive with a wonderful deliverance."
Joseph comforted his brothers for what they had done.
"Now, see, it was not you who sent me out here
But the supreme God who made me into a father for Pharaoh
And master of his entire household, and
Ruler of the whole land of Egypt.
As for you, who acted to injure me and my father,
I have seen how greatly you have repented,
For you were ready to become my slaves so that
My father should not be bereft of Benjamin as he was of me.
My father will forgive you as I have forgiven you.
He will see that the hand of God was in this.
Be quick, go up to my father and say to him,
Thus says your son, Joseph, 'God has made me
Master of all Egypt, come down to me. Do not delay.
You shall live in the land of Goshen; you will be near to me,
You, your children and your children's children,
Your flocks and your herds and all that you possess.
There will I support you for there remain five years of famine,
Otherwise you will be destitute, you and your household
And all that belongs to you.' And behold your eyes tell you,
As do the eyes of Benjamin, that it is I who speak to you.
I, Joseph, your brother! You will tell my father of all my
Glory in the land of Egypt, and all that you have seen.
You will make haste to bring down my father to this place."
He fell on the neck of Benjamin, his brother, and wept.

And Benjamin wept on his brother's neck.
Joseph was then thirty-nine years old when he
Made himself known to Benjamin and his brothers.

He kissed every one of his brothers and wept with them.
Only afterwards were his brothers able to speak to him,
So shocked were they by all that had happened to them
Since they first came down to Egypt.
They understood why their money had been returned
And why the cup had been put into Benjamin's sack,
For Joseph their brother had tested them.
They spoke on these matters while they ate and drank.

Reports of Joseph and his brothers reached Pharaoh's palace,
"The brothers of Joseph have come here."
This pleased Pharaoh and his ministers.
Pharaoh said to Joseph, "Say this to your brothers.
This is what you shall do. Load up your beasts and go.
Get you to the land of Canaan, fetch your father and
Your families and come here. I will give you
The best of the land of Egypt and you will
Eat of the fat of the land. You are commanded to do this.
Take your wagons from the land of Egypt for your little ones,
Your wives, and fetch your father and return.
Also, let your eyes have no regard for your possessions,
Because the best of the land shall be yours."

I will go and see him before I die

The sons of Israel did this. Joseph gave them wagons
According to Pharaoh's command and
Provisions for the journey.
To each of them, he gave a new change of clothes but to
Benjamin he gave three hundred pieces of silver and
Five changes of clothing. To his father he sent this:
Ten donkeys laden with the finest things of Egypt and ten
Donkeys bearing grain, bread and food for his father's journey.

He sent off his brothers and they were ready to go.
He said to them, "Do not fall out with each other
On the way!"
For he knew that the events had confused them
And they would not know what to say to their father.

They departed from Egypt and arrived in the land of Canaan
To Jacob their father. They told him the news:
"Joseph is alive.
He rules over the whole breadth of the land of Egypt."
His heart faltered because he could not believe them.
They told him all that Joseph had said to them.
When he saw the wagons which Joseph had sent to carry him,
The spirit of Jacob their father revived. Israel declared,
"It is enough. I **believe it**. Joseph my son is alive.
I will go and see him before I die."

Israel set out with all his property and came to Beersheba.
He offered up sacrifices to the God of his father Isaac.
God said to Israel in the visions of the night,
He said to him, "Jacob, Jacob." He answered, "Here am I."
He said, "I am the God, the god of your father.
Do not be afraid to go down to Egypt,
For there I will make them into a great nation.
I will go down with you to Egypt.
I will also surely bring you up from there,
When you die, Joseph will put his hands on your eyes."

Israel left Beersheba and the sons of Israel
Set out with Jacob, their father, their little ones and wives
In the wagons which Pharaoh had sent to carry them.
They took their cattle and the possessions which
They had got in the land of Canaan.
They came to Egypt; Jacob and all his descendants with him.
He brought with him his children, his children's children and
All his descendants to Egypt.
And the names of the sons of Israel who went to

Egypt were written in the Book of Genealogies.[1]
All the persons who came to be in Egypt numbered seventy.

He sent Judah ahead of him to Joseph
To show him the way to Goshen.
They came to the land of Goshen.
Joseph had his chariot made ready.
He went up to meet Israel, his father, in Goshen.
He presented himself to his father.
He fell upon his neck and wept
On his neck for a very long time.
Israel said to Joseph,
"Now I can die for I have seen your face,
That you are alive!"

Joseph said to his brothers, and to his father's household,
"I will go up and tell Pharaoh and say to him,
'My brothers and my father's household from
The land of Canaan have come to me.
The men are shepherds for they have kept cattle.
They have brought their flocks and herds.
All that they own they have brought.'
Now when Pharaoh calls to see you,
He will ask, 'What is your trade?'
You answer, 'Your servants have kept cattle since our youth
Even until now, not only us but also our ancestors'."
This you must say, so that you may dwell in Goshen
For all shepherds are abhorrent to the Egyptians'."

Joseph went in and told Pharaoh the news.
"My father, my brothers, their flocks and herds,
All they possess, have arrived from the land of Canaan.
They are now in the land of Goshen."
From among his brothers he chose five of them and
Introduced them to Pharaoh. Pharaoh said to his brothers,

---

[1] See appendix 5; for Genesis 46:8–27

"What is your trade?" They replied to Pharaoh,
"Your servants are shepherds, as were our ancestors."
They said to Pharaoh, "We have come to settle in the land
Because there is no pasture for your servants' flocks
For the famine is severe in the land of Canaan.
We beg of you, let your servants settle in the land of Goshen."
Pharaoh said to Joseph, "Your father and brothers
Have come to you. The land of Egypt is before you,
In the best part of the country settle your father and brothers,
Let them dwell in the land of Goshen.
If you know any skilful men among them,
Put them in charge over my cattle."

Joseph brought Jacob his father to introduce him to Pharaoh,
Jacob blessed Pharaoh. Pharaoh asked Jacob,
"How many are the years of your life?"
Jacob answered Pharaoh, "The days of the years of
My sojournings are one hundred and thirty.
Few and wearisome have been the days of the years
Of my life. They have not attained the years
Of life reached by my ancestors during their sojournings."
Jacob blessed Pharaoh and went out from Pharaoh's presence.
Joseph settled his father and his brothers, giving them
Possession of part of the land of Egypt
In the choicest district of Rameses as Pharaoh had ordered.
Joseph sustained his father and his brothers,
Every member of his father's household, with food
As much as they and every child required.

Buy us and our land for food

There was no food in the whole country because
The famine was so severe, so that the land of Egypt and
The land of Canaan were devastated because of the famine.
Joseph had collected all the money that was available
In the land of Egypt and in the land of Canaan

As the price for the grain which they bought from him.
Joseph brought the money into Pharaoh's palace.
When all the money had been spent in the land of Egypt
And in the land of Canaan, all the Egyptians
Came to Joseph **and his agents,** pleading, "Give us bread,
Why should we die before you, for we have no money."
Joseph said, "Bring your livestock, and I will give you grain
For the livestock if you have no money."
They brought their livestock to Joseph. He gave them food
In exchange for horses, the flocks, the herds and the donkeys.
That year he provided them with food in exchange for
All their livestock. When that year ended,
They came to him in the following year and said to him,
"We cannot hide from my lord that our money is gone,
All our livestock are now our master's.
Nothing remains for us before my master
Except our bodies and our lands.
Why should we perish before you, we and our lands?
Buy us and our land for food. We, with our lands,
Will become slaves to Pharaoh. Give us seed,
That we may live and not die and the
Land not become desolate."
Joseph thus bought the whole land of Egypt for Pharaoh.
Because the Egyptians – every man – sold his fields as
The famine was so intense for them.
The land became Pharaoh's. As for the people, he moved
Them about to different places of settlement
From one end of the border to the other end
So that they would be far from the land they once owned.
Priestly lands he did not buy because it was the
Privilege of the priests awarded by Pharaoh
To eat of the portions that Pharaoh gave them.
For this reason they did not need to sell their land.
Joseph declared to the people, "I have bought your land
For Pharaoh today. Here is seed, sow the ground.
When you come to harvest, you will give a fifth to Pharaoh,

Four fifths will belong to you, to seed the field,
And for your food, for the members of your household
And for your little ones." They said,
"You have saved our lives; may it please our lord,
We will be Pharaoh's serfs." The tax structure that
Joseph established in the land of Egypt exists to this day:
Pharaoh receives a fifth of the produce,
Only the lands of the priests do not belong to Pharaoh.

Israel was living in the land of Egypt
In the district of Goshen and bought property there.
They were fruitful and their numbers increased exceedingly.
Jacob lived in the land of Egypt for seventeen years.
The years of Jacob's life were
One hundred and forty-seven years.
The time of Israel's death approached,
He called his son, Joseph.
He said to him, "If you would be gracious to me,
Put your hand under my thigh and perform for me
An act of true kindness: do not bury me in Egypt.
When I sleep with my fathers, bear me out of Egypt,
Bury me in their burial ground." He said,
"I will do what you ask." He said, "Swear this to me."
He took an oath. Israel, then from the head of his bed,
Bowed **in gratitude for the oath that Joseph had taken.**[1]

After these events, Joseph was told, "Your father is not well."
He took his two sons with him, Menasseh and Ephraim.
Jacob was told, "Your son Joseph has come to see you."
Israel mustered his strength to sit up in bed.
Jacob said to Joseph, "God Shaddai appeared to me in Luz
In the land of Canaan and he blessed me.

---

[1] Why did Jacob ask Joseph for an oath? Was not his promise sufficient? As later developments will indicate, there may have been a new Pharaoh who no longer favoured Joseph, and the request to leave Egypt to bury Jacob may have been refused. For this reason, Jacob wants an oath that guarantees that Joseph will not rest until he has achieved Jacob's dying wish.

He said to me, 'Behold, I will make you fruitful and
Make you increase into a community of nations.
I will give this land to your descendants after you for an
Eternal possession.' Now your two sons who were born
To you in the land of Egypt before I came to you,
They shall be mine. Ephraim and Menasseh, even as
Reuben and Simeon, **my first born sons,** shall be mine,
Your children which you may sire after them are yours,
But their inheritance will be with their two brothers
**Equally with my other sons who will share in the
Land of Canaan.**
I do this because of my love for your mother Rachel.
When I returned from Paddan, Rachel died as I held her,
In the land of Canaan, some way before Ephrath.
I buried her there on the road to Ephrath [Bethlehem].

Then Israel dimly saw the sons of Joseph. He asked,
"Who are these men?" Joseph answered his father,
"They are my sons, whom God gave me in this place."
He said, "Bring them close to me and I will bless them."
The eyes of Israel were very dim through old age,
So that he could not see. He brought them nearer to him.
He kissed and embraced them. Israel said to Joseph,
"I had not thought that I would see your face again,
And see God has even made me to see your children."
Then, removing them from his knees, Joseph
Bowed himself, with his face to the ground.

Joseph then took both of them, Ephraim by his right hand
Towards Israel's left and Menasseh by his left hand
Towards Israel's right. Thus he brought them close to him,
So that when Jacob blessed them,
He would put his right hand
On his first born's head and his left on Ephraim's.
Israel stretched out his right hand and placed it on
The head of Ephraim, who was the younger one and
His left hand on the head of Menasseh, crossing

His hands intentionally for Menasseh was the first born.
He blessed Joseph, "The God before whom my fathers walked,
Abraham and Isaac, the God who was my shepherd
All my life until this very day. The Messengers of God
Who delivered me from all trouble will bless the boys.
They will carry on my name[1]
And the name of Abraham and Isaac.
May they grow into a multitude on the earth."
Joseph saw that his father had placed his right hand on
The head of Ephraim and it did not please him.
He lifted his father's hand to remove it from Ephraim's head
To put it on Menasseh's head. Joseph said,
"Not so, my father,
This one is the first born. Place your right hand on his head."
His father refused, "I know, my son, I know.
He too will become a great nation; he too will be great,
But his younger brother will be greater than he,
And his descendants will be a multitude of nations."
He also blessed them on that day, "By you
shall the people of Israel bless themselves with these words,
'May God make you as Ephraim and Menasseh.'"
Thus, he set Ephraim before Menasseh, the first born.[2]

Israel said to Joseph, "Look, I am about to die,
God be with you and bring you back to your ancestral land.
I will bestow upon you one portion
More than your brothers which I took from the Amorites
With the power of my sword and bow."[3]

---

[1] By adopting Ephraim and Menasseh as his two sons, Jacob gives Joseph a double portion in the division of Canaan following the conquests of the Promised Land. There will now be thirteen tribes rather than twelve. Because the tribe of Levi, being the Priestly caste, were given no land, one still speaks of the Twelve Tribes.

[2] The constant preference of the younger to the first born in Genesis would suggest an attack on the tradition of primogeniture, when the elder received a double inheritance.

[3] He is now looking into the future when the Israelites will conquer Canaan.

On his death bed Jacob called his sons,
"Gather yourselves together and I will tell you
What will happen to you in the days to come."
When they arrived at his bedside, he said:
"Sons of Jacob, gather yourselves around and
Hear the voice of Israel your father.

"Reuben, you are my first born,
My strength, the first fruits of my potency
Therefore, superior in status and authority
But, volatile as water, you have forfeited your rank.
You went into your father's concubine.
To my shame, you have mounted my couch.

"Simeon and Levi are true brothers,
Weapons of violence are their profession.
Let not my person be mentioned in their councils.
To their communities, let not my reputation be joined!
In their anger they killed people
And gratuitously they ham-strung oxen.[1]
Cursed be their anger because of its intensity
And their wrath because of its cruelty.
I will divide them throughout Jacob
And scatter them throughout Israel.

"Judah, you are praised by your brothers.
Your hand will hold the neck of your enemies,
Your father's sons will bow down to you.
Judah is a lion's whelp.
After the prey, you go up to the hills.
He crouches, he crouches as a lion
And like a mighty lioness –

[1] It was the custom to do this to weaken the enemy animals of transport. To do this to the animals they looted from Shechem was perverse. The reader should note how, in this and the previous blessing, Jacob vents his anger over events for which he remained silent when they occurred. Because Levi had no allotted land, he would not be able to join up with Simeon.

Who dare arouse him?
The sceptre shall not pass on from Judah
And the staff of sovereignty from between his feet,
So that tributes will come to him
To him will the peoples submit.
He harnesses his foal for the produce of one vine,
His ass's colt for the produce of one choice vine.
He washes his clothes in wine,
His robe in the blood of grapes.
His eyes are as sparkling as wine,
His teeth whiter than milk.

"Zebulun shall dwell by the sea coast.
He shall be a haven for ships.
His border shall stretch to Sidon.

"Issacher is as a strong-boned donkey
Lying down among the sheepfolds.
When he saw how good was security
And how pleasant was the land,
He put his back into his work
And became a hard-working serf.

"Dan shall defend his people
As one of the tribes of Israel.
Dan shall be a serpent in the way,
A viper in the path
That bites the horse's heels,
So that his rider topples backwards.
I await your deliverance for him, O LORD.

"Gad, raiders shall press hard upon him,
But he will press hard upon their heels in return.

"Asher's bread will be rich
His land will yield delicacies fit for kings.

"Naphtali is a hind let loose,
Which brings forth lovely fawns.

"Joseph is a fruitful tree,
A fruitful tree by a spring,
Whose branches climb over the wall.
The archers have harassed him,
Drew their bows and attacked him.
Yet his bow remained firm
His arms and his hands were strengthened
By the Mighty One of Jacob –
There by the shepherd, the Rock of Israel.
Your father's God who helps you,
And Shaddai who blesses you
With the blessings from heaven above,
With blessings from the depths below –
Blessings of the breasts and the womb,
The blessings of your father upon you
Surpass the blessings of my parents.
The blessings of eternal heights
May they be on the head of Joseph,
On the crown of the prince of his brothers.

"Benjamin is a ravenous wolf.
In the morning he consumes,
In the evening he shares out the spoils."

Bury me with my fathers

All these are the twelve tribes of Israel.
This was what their father said when he blessed them,
Each man according to his blessing did he bless them.
He charged them, "I am to be gathered to my people.
Bury me with my fathers in the cave of the
Field of Ephron the Hittite,
In the cave that is in the field of Machpelah
Which faces Mamre in the land of Canaan,
The field which Abraham brought from
Ephron the Hittite for a permanent burial site.

There they buried Abraham and Sarah,
His wife; there they buried Isaac and Rebecca, his wife.
There I buried Leah, in the field and its cave
Which was purchased from the Hittites."
When Jacob finished these instructions to his sons
He drew his feet into the bed and, breathing his last,
He was gathered to his people.

Joseph fell upon his father's face, wept for him and kissed him.
Joseph ordered his physicians to embalm his father.
The physicians embalmed Jacob. It took forty days for him,
For that is the period required for embalming.
The Egyptians mourned for him seventy days.
When the period of mourning had passed,
Joseph petitioned the ministers of Pharaoh, "If I please you,
I implore you to say this in the ears of Pharaoh,
'My father made me swear to him by saying to me,
'See, I am about to die. In the grave I prepared for myself
In the land of Canaan, there shall you bury me.
Now, allow me to go up and bury my father.
Then I will return.'" **Joseph did not speak to Pharaoh,
Because he was no longer second to him in ruling Egypt.**
Pharaoh agreed: "Go up and bury your father
As he has made you swear."
So Joseph went up to bury his father.
All the ministers of Pharaoh,
The elders of his household and all
The elders of the land of Egypt went up with him. The whole
House of Joseph and his brothers and his father's household,
Only their little ones and their flocks and herds
Were left in Goshen.
**For Pharaoh was afraid that the Israelites would leave Egypt
If they took their little ones and their livestock with them.**
Chariots as well as horsemen went up with him.
The company was very great. **Pharaoh sent his elders
And his troops to show off his glory to the people of Canaan,**

To guard the people of Israel and bring them back to Egypt.[1]
When they came to Goren Ha-atad
Which was across the Jordan,"
There they wailed with great and loud lamentations.
He observed a mourning period of seven days for his father.
When the inhabitants of Canaan witnessed the lamenting
In Goren Ha-atad, they remarked, "This is an occasion for
Serious mourning for Egypt." So the name of it was called
Abel-Mizraim[2] which is across the Jordan.

His sons then did for him as he had ordered them –
His sons carried him to the land of Canaan and
Buried him in the cave of the field of Machpelah,
The field which Abraham purchased
For a permanent burial place
From Ephron the Hittite, before the approach to Mamre.

Then Joseph returned to Egypt, he and his brothers and
All those who went up with him to bury his father.
After they buried his father, the brothers of Joseph were afraid,
Because their father was dead, for they said,
"Joseph may still hate us. **While our father was alive
He would do us no harm because of his respect for him.**
Now he will seek recompense from us
For the evil we did to him."
They sent him this message, "Before his death your father
Made this command: 'Thus shall you say to Joseph,
'Forgive, I ask of you the transgressions of your brothers,
And their sins for they behaved wickedly towards you.

[1] Joseph's promise to return to Egypt and the notice that the little ones and the livestock remained in Goshen, would indicate that the captivity of the Israelites told at the beginning of Exodus had already begun while Joseph was still alive and still yielding some influence at Pharaoh's court. This is the justification for my interactions with the original text.

[2] English meaning is 'the Mourning of Egypt'. The alternative name for Goren Ha-atad may have been the inspiration for this aspect of the story of Jacob's burial. There is no plausible explanation for the entourage to have stopped for a period of seven days' mourning before they arrived at the burial place.

Now, please forgive the transgression of the servants of
The God of your fathers."' Joseph wept at their words to him,
For he knew that Jacob had never said such things but
That they feared for their lives after their father's death.
His brothers also went to him and fell before him, saying,
"Here, let us be your slaves." But Joseph said to them,
"Do not be afraid, for am I in the place of God!
It was your intention to harm me,
But God turned it to good, so that he could bring about this:
The survival of many people. Now do not be afraid,
I will still support you and your little ones."
So did he comfort them and put their minds at rest.

Joseph dwelt in Egypt, he and his father's house.
Joseph lived to be a hundred and ten years old.
Joseph lived to see Ephraim's children to the third generation,
The children of Machir, the son of Menasseh, were also
Born upon Joseph's knees. And Joseph said to his brothers,[1]
"I am about to die. God will certainly remember you,
To bring you up from this land to the land
Which he promised to Abraham, Isaac and Jacob."
Joseph made the children of Israel take an oath:
"When God remembers you, to bring you out of Egypt,
You will carry up my bones from this place."
Joseph died at the age of one hundred and ten years.
They embalmed him and placed him in a coffin in

Egypt.

[1] The period between Jacob's and Joseph's death was according to the text
fifty-four years. By this time, Joseph had no influence to persuade the Pharaoh
to allow him to be buried in Canaan as he or the previous Pharaoh had
permitted to Jacob. Indeed, by this time the oppression of the Israelites had
become severe. Thus Joseph's promise of God's deliverance from Egypt.

APPENDIX ONE

Descendants of Japheth   *Genesis 10:2–5*
The sons of Japheth were Gomer, Magog, Madai,
Javan, Tubal, Meshech and Tiras.
The sons of Gomer were Ashkenaz, Ripath and Togarmah.
The sons of Javan: Elishah, Tarshish, Kittim, and Dodanim.
Among these were the coastlands of the nations divided in
Their lands, every one according to his language
According to their clans in their nations.

Descendants of Ham   *Genesis 10:6–20*
Cush, Mizraim, Put and Canaan
The sons of Cush: Seba, Havila, Sabta, Raamah and Sabteca.
The sons of Raamah: Sheba and Dedan.
Cush sired Nimrod: He was the first of the mighty men on
        earth.
He was a hero of the chase before the Lord; therefore one
        says,
"Like Nimrod, a hero of the chase before the Lord."
Babylon was the beginning of his kingdom and also
Erech; Accad and Calneh in the land of Sumeria.
Out of that land he went forth to conquer Assyria and
Built Nineveh and Rehoboth-Ir [Expansive City] and Calah
And Resen he built between Nineveh and Calah –
All three are the great city.

Mizraim sired Ludim, Anamim, Lehabim, Naphtuhim,
Pathrusim, Casluhim [ancestors of the Philistines], Caphtorim.
Canaan sired Zidon, his firstborn, and Heth, the Jebusites,
The Amorites and the Girgashites, the Hivites, the
Arkites, the Sinites, the Arvadites,
The Zemarites and the Hamathites.
Afterwards, the clans of the Canaanites spread out.
The Canaanite border extended from Zidon towards Gerar
Up to Gaza and towards Sodom and Gemorrah and
Admah and Zeboiim up to Lasha.

These are the sons of Ham, according to their clans and
Languages by their lands and nations.

The Descendants of Shem   *Genesis 10:21–32*
To Shem, the elder brother of Japheth and the
Ancestor of all the children of Eber [his great-grandson],
To him also were sons born: the sons of Shem:
Elam, Asshur, Archpashad, Lud and Aram.
The sons of Aram: Uz, Hul, Gether and Mash.
Archpashad sired Shelah; Shelah sired Eber. To
Eber were born two sons: the name of one was Peleg [Division]
For in his days was the land divided into canals.
His brother's name was Joktan. Joktan sired
Almodad, Sheleph, Hazarmaveth and Jerah,
Hadoram, Uzal, Dikla, Obal, Abimael and Sheba,
Ophir, Havilah and Jobab. All these were the sons of Joktan.
The territory in which they lived extended from Mesha
Towards Sephar, the mountain range of the east.
These are the sons of Shem according to their clans,
Their languages in their lands and nations.
These are the clans of the sons of Noah, according to their
Genealogies in their nations. And from these other
Nations branched out over the earth after the flood.

APPENDIX TWO

Descendants of Abraham by Keturah   *Genesis 25:2–5*
She bore him Zimram, Jokshan, Medan,
Midian, Ishbak and Shua.
Jokshan sired Sheba and Dedan. The sons of Dedan were
Asshurim, Letushim and Leummim.
The sons of Midian were Ephah, Epher,
Hanoch, Abidah and Eldaah.
All these were the descendants of Keturah.

APPENDIX THREE

The Descendants of Ishmael   *Genesis 25:13*
These are the names of the descendants of Ishmael
According to name and genealogy.
The firstborn of Ishmael was Nebaioth,
Then Kedar, Adbeel, Mibsam, Mishma, Dumah, Massa;
Hadad, Tema, Jetur, Naphish and Kedmah.
These are the twelve sons of Ishmael and these are their names
According to their villages and encampments.
Twelve princes with as many tribes.

APPENDIX FOUR

The Descendants of Esau   *Genesis 36:9–19*
These are the genealogies of Esau, the ancestor of the
Edomites in Mount Seir. These are the names of Esau's sons:
Eliphaz, the son of Adah the wife of Esau
Reuel, the son of Basemath, the wife of Esau
The sons of Eliphaz were Teman, Omar, Zepho,
Gatam and Kenaz.
Timna was concubine to Eliphaz [Esau's son].
She bore to Eliphaz Amalek.
These are the descendants of Adah.
These are the sons of Reuel: Nahath,
Zerah, Shammah and Mizzah.
These are the descendants of Basemath [Esau's wife].
These are the sons of Oholibamah [the daughter of Anah,
The daughter of Zibeon, Esau's wife]. She bore to Esau
Jeush, Jalam and Korah. These are the military chieftains of
The descendants of Esau: the descendants of Eliphaz,
[Firstborn of Esau] chieftain of Teman, chieftain of Omar,
Chieftain of Zepho, chieftain of Kenaz, chieftain of Korah,
Chieftain of Gatam, chieftain of Amalek: these are the
Chieftains that descended from Eliphaz in the land of Edom;

These are the sons of Adah. These are the sons of Reuel,
Esau's son: chieftain of Nahath, chieftain of Zerah,
Chieftain of Shammah, chieftain of Mizzah: these are the
Chieftains that descended from Reuel in the land of Edom;
These are the sons of Basemath, Esau's wife.
These are the sons of Oholibamah, Esau's wife: the
Chieftain of Jeush, the chieftain of Jalam, the chieftain of
Korah: these are the chieftains that came of
Oholibamah, the daughter of Anah, Esau's wife.
These are the sons of Esau, and these are their
Chieftains: Esau is known as Edom.

The Descendants of Seir the Horite   *Genesis 36:20–30*
The inhabitants of the land **before Esau's clans settled there:**
Lotan, Shobal, Zibeon, Anah, Dishon, Ezer and Dishan.
These are the chieftains that descended from the Horites,
The descendants of Seir in the land of Edom.
The sons of Lotan were Hori and Hemam and
Lotan's sister was Timna. These are the sons of Shobal:
Alvan, Menahath, Ebal, Shepho and Onam.
These are the sons of Zibeon:
Aiah and Anah: This is the Anah who found
Hot springs in the wilderness as he fed the donkeys of
Zibeon, his father. These are the children of Anah:
Dishon and Oholibamah [Esau's wife], the daughter of Anah.
These are the sons of Dishon: Hemdan, Eshban,
Ithran and Cheran.
These are the sons of Ezer: Bilhan, Zaavan and Akan.
These are the sons of Dishan: Uz and Aran.
These are the chieftains that descended from the Horites:
The chieftains of Lotan, Shobal, Zibeon, Anah, Dishon,
Ezer and Dishan. These are the chieftains that
Descended from the Horites according
To their clans in the land of Seir.

The Kings of Edom before the Kingdom of Israel
and Judah *Genesis 36:31–39*
These are the kings that reigned in the land of Edom
Before there reigned any king over the Children of Israel.
Bela the son of Beor reigned in Edom –
The name of his city was Dinhabah.
When Bela died, Jobab son of Zerah of Bozrah succeeded him.
When Jobab died, Husham of the land of the Temanites
Succeeded him. When Husham died, Hadad the son of Belad
Who defeated Midian in the fields of Moab succeeded him.
His city was called Avith. When Hedad died, Samlah of
Masrekah succeeded him. When Samlah died,
Shaul of Rehoboth by the River succeeded him as king.
When Shaul died, Baal-Hanan the son of Achbor
Reigned in his place. When Baal-Hanan son of Achbor died,
Hadar succeeded him. His city was called Pau.
His wife's name was Mehetabel, the daughter of Matred,
The daughter of Me-za-hab.

The Chieftains of the Edomites *Genesis 36:40–43*
These are the names of the chieftains descended from Esau
According to their clans, and their localities by their names:
The chieftains of Timnah, Alvah, Jetheth, Oholibamah,
Elah, Pinon, Kenaz, Teman, Mibzar, Magdiel and Iram.
These then are the chieftains of Edom, according to
Their settlements in the land they possessed.
This is Esau the father of the Edomites.

APPENDIX FIVE

The Descendants of Israel *Genesis 46:8–27*
These are the names of the sons of Israel who came to Egypt;
Jacob and his sons: Reuben, Jacob's firstborn.
The sons of Reuben: Hanoch, Pallu, Hezron and Carmi.
The sons of Simeon: Jemuel, Jamin, Ohad, Jachin, Zohar
And Shaul, the son of the Canaanite woman.

The sons of Levi: Gershon, Kohath and Merari.
The sons of Judah:Er, Onan, Shelah, Perez and Zerah.
But Er and Onan died in the land of Canaan.
The sons of Perez were Hezron and Hamul.
The sons of Issacher: Tola, Puvah,Iob and Shimron.
The sons of Zebulun: Sered, Elon and Jahleel.
These are the sons of Leah which she bore for
Jacob in Paddan Aram with his daughter Dinah.
All these sons and daughter numbered thirty-three.[1]

The sons of Gad: Ziphion, Haggi, Shuni, Ezbon, Eri, Arodi,
    Areli.
The sons of Asher: Imnah, Ishvah, Ishvi, Beriah, and Serah,
Their sister. The sons of Beriah: Heber and Malchiel.
These are the descendants of Zilpah whom Laban gave to
Leah his daughter; these she bore to Jacob – sixteen children.

The sons of Rachel, Jacob's wife: Joseph and Benjamin.
To Joseph in the land of Egypt were born Menasseh and Ephraim
Whom Asenath, the daughter of Poti-phera, priest of On,
Bore for him. The sons of Benjamin: Bela, Becher,
Ashbel, Gera, Naaman, Ehi, Rosh, Muppim, Huppim and Ard.[2]
These are the descendants of Rachel
Which were born to Jacob: fourteen.

The son of Dan: Hushim.
The sons of Naphtali: Jahzeel, Guni, Jezer and Shillem.
These are the descendants of Bilhah whom Laban gave to
Rachel, his daughter. These she bore for Jacob: seven.

All the persons that came with Jacob into Egypt,
Who came out of his loins, besides Jacob's sons' wives[3], were

---

[1] The number is thirty-three only if one includes Jacob.

[2] The ten children sired by Benjamin while in Canaan would indicate that he was not just a lad. In fact, Genesis gives us evidence that Benjamin would have been thirty-six to thirty-seven years old. While mature, he was still Jacob's 'baby' and was considered as such by his brothers.

[3] Were Jacob's wife Leah and the two concubines alive but not numbered? While there is no report of Leah's death, Jacob later tells us that he buried

Sixty-six. Add to this the two sons who were born
To Joseph in Egypt. **Counting Joseph and Jacob,**
All the persons of Jacob's house who came to Egypt
Or who were already there numbered seventy.

her in the Cave in Machpelah, so she would have died before the migration to
Egypt. Zilpah and Bilhah may have been alive but were not considered worthy
of being counted. The mention of two daughters, Jacob's and Asher's, is
noteworthy. Could they be supposed according to the author to be the only
daughters born to the Patriarch and his twelve sons. Two out of sixty-nine
(Jacob makes the number seventy) seems a ridiculously small proportion of
female births. The assumption is that, consistent with the patriarchal view of
society, women are not mentioned except when they play a role. Dinah does,
Serah, Asher's daughter, does not. It is a mystery.